A Conceptual History of Psychophysics

Nicola Bruno

A Conceptual History of Psychophysics

Ernst Weber's Law of Desire

Nicola Bruno
Dipartimento di Neuroscienze
Universita di Parma
Parma, Italy

ISBN 978-3-031-66596-7   ISBN 978-3-031-66597-4 (eBook)
https://doi.org/10.1007/978-3-031-66597-4

© The Editor(s) (if applicable) and The Author(s), under exclusive licence to Springer Nature Switzerland AG 2024

Translation from the Italian language edition: "La Legge Del Desiderio" by Julie Wood and Nicola Bruno, © Il Mulino 2023. Published by Il Mulino. All Rights Reserved.
This work is subject to copyright. All rights are solely and exclusively licensed by the Publisher, whether the whole or part of the material is concerned, specifically the rights of reprinting, reuse of illustrations, recitation, broadcasting, reproduction on microfilms or in any other physical way, and transmission or information storage and retrieval, electronic adaptation, computer software, or by similar or dissimilar methodology now known or hereafter developed.
The use of general descriptive names, registered names, trademarks, service marks, etc. in this publication does not imply, even in the absence of a specific statement, that such names are exempt from the relevant protective laws and regulations and therefore free for general use.
The publisher, the authors and the editors are safe to assume that the advice and information in this book are believed to be true and accurate at the date of publication. Neither the publisher nor the authors or the editors give a warranty, expressed or implied, with respect to the material contained herein or for any errors or omissions that may have been made. The publisher remains neutral with regard to jurisdictional claims in published maps and institutional affiliations.

This Palgrave Macmillan imprint is published by the registered company Springer Nature Switzerland AG.
The registered company address is: Gewerbestrasse 11, 6330 Cham, Switzerland

If disposing of this product, please recycle the paper.

Contents

1 "To investigate the essence, I take it to be an impossible endeavour" 1

2 The Marriage of Heaven and Hell 7

3 The Doors of Perception 31

4 The Calculus of Desire 51

5 Epilogue 69

Index 73

List of Figures

Fig. 2.1 Four squares containing 10, 20, 110, and 120 dots. The difference between 20 and 10 dots is equal to the difference between 110 and 120. But in the first case, there clearly seems to be more dots in the lower square than in the upper square. In the second case, on the other hand, there seems to be the same number in each square. In the first case, therefore, the increase of 10 dots allows us to notice the difference, while in the second case a larger increase would be necessary. This is precisely Weber's Law. *Source*: Wikimedia Commons CC BY-SA 4.0 (image in the public domain) 11

Fig. 2.2 Fechner's Law for the sensation of weight, assuming that Weber's constant ratio between threshold and intensity is equal to 0.05 and that the absolute threshold is equal to 12.5 grams. The "units of sensation" on the y-axis are arbitrary. Note that equal ratios between weights on the x-axis correspond to equal differences in sensations on the y-axis 14

Fig. 2.3 Left: Psychophysical functions for the sensations of sound intensity (exponent 0.33), visual length of a segment (straight line in grey, exponent 1), and intensity of an electric shock (exponent 3.5), according to Stevens. The curves are drawn assuming that I is measured in the same arbitrary units. Right: the same functions redrawn after the log transformation of both axes. The slopes of the three lines correspond to the exponents of the original functions 23

Fig. 2.4 The magnitude estimation method applied to measuring pain. The patient is asked to mark the intensity of the sensation on a scale of 1–10 24

viii LIST OF FIGURES

Fig. 3.1   The results of one of Pirenne's experimental sessions. In each trial, the participant saw one of six possible discs illuminated with 47, 73, 114, 178, 276, or 421 light quanta. The dots show the proportion of "yes" answers (the participant states that they saw the disc) according to these six levels of intensity. The S-shaped curve is fitted to the six dots to estimate the proportions for all the other possible intensity values on the x-axis. This curve, known in psychophysics as the *psychometric function*, represents the correct way of defining the concept of threshold in psychophysics: as a mathematical model of uncertainty   37

Fig. 3.2   Phantom vibration in Fechner's inner psychophysics. Imagine two different situations: in the first (top line) there is no vibration; in the second (bottom line), there is a vibration with intensity A. The curves represent the variability of internal activation, given by the value of the physical vibration (top, 0; below, A, shown by the dotted segments) plus the random variability of the neural signals. The area below the "Gaussian" bell-shaped curve represents the relative probability of the magnitude of the error. Fechner proposed that there is conscious sensation when internal activations exceed the intermediate value between the peaks of the two distributions ($d/2$, i.e., the average of the activations in the two cases, the dotted segments). In this way, the grey area to the right of $d/2$ in the two curves represents the probability of an activation above that reference level. If the vibration is actually present (bottom curve), the model predicts that this activation will produce a real sensation. If it is absent (top curve), the model predicts that it will produce a phantom vibration   44

Fig. 4.1   The phenomenon of risk aversion is explained by the concave shape (similar to that of Fechner's function) of the curve. You can see that the subjective value of the risky choice corresponds to the sum of the subjective values of the two options (2100 Euros or nothing, dotted horizontal lines) multiplied by their probability (50%). Note that this value lies exactly half-way between the subjective value of a €2100 salary and a €0 salary, if these were certain. For this reason, the subjective value of the risky choice, for a person whose curve has this shape, becomes much less than that of the safe choice   56

Fig. 4.2   Three types of attitude to risk shown by three types of subjective value curve. Suppose you have to choose between two alternatives with the same expected salary: a sure salary of

	€1000 and a salary of €2000 with a probability of 50%. With a concave curve, the subjective value of the risky option lies below that of the safe option. A person with this attitude will be averse to risk. With a straight line, the subjective value of the risky option is equal to the monetary value. This person is indifferent to the two options. With a convex curve, the subjective value of the risky option lies above that of the safe option. This person is inclined to risk	57
Fig. 4.3	Prospect theory. Subjective value is a sigmoid function of monetary value, but disappointment grows faster in the negative quadrant of the plot than satisfaction increases in the positive quadrant. Note that (1) the satisfaction associated with an increase from the reference level to B is only slightly higher than the increase from the reference to A (Weber's Law); (2) the disappointment associated with losing –A is higher, as an absolute value, than the satisfaction associated with gaining A (loss aversion); (3) a certain disadvantageous outcome V(A) has higher subjective value than a risky alternative V(B or 0) in which one may gain B or nothing (risk aversion in a gain context); (4) the subjective disappointment associated to a risky alternative V(–B or 0) is less than that of a certain outcome V(–A) (risk propensity in a loss context)	61

CHAPTER 1

"To investigate the essence, I take it to be an impossible endeavour"

Abstract Here I introduce my story of conceptual interdisciplinary connections, impacting fields as diverse as psychology, cognitive neuroscience, economics, and everyday behaviours. A conceptual history of psychophysics, a relatively unknown but fundamental discipline, showing how early insights into sensation measurement evolved into modern theories of decision-making and a Nobel prize in economics. An unusual approach to desire, defined as a mental content whose intensity drives preferences between alternatives.

Keywords Desire • Psychophysics • Sensation • Experimental psychology • Economics

We are all familiar with desire. We encounter it all the time in our lives. For the scientist, however, dealing with desire is far from easy. Where does the problem lie? Consulting a dictionary, we will find a definition that reads more or less like this: "a feeling of wanting to have something, or of wishing for something to happen". Desire is what makes the grocery shopper in the supermarket put that one product in the trolley, rather than any of the others displayed on the shelf.

© The Author(s), under exclusive license to Springer Nature Switzerland AG 2024
N. Bruno, *A Conceptual History of Psychophysics*,
https://doi.org/10.1007/978-3-031-66597-4_1

But for the Spanish film director Pedro Almodovar, desire is that overwhelming drive that dictates the actions of Antonio, Juan, and Pablo, the protagonists of the unforgettable love triangle that shapes the film script of *Law of Desire*,[1] driving the first towards evermore extreme choices—as far as murder and then suicide—and the second towards a sorrowful flight, while the third remains unable to commit in one direction or the other. For the psychoanalyst Jacques Lacan, desire is the "metonymy of the lack of being",[2] the subconscious force that relates us to others who are not here, but we would like them to be. What we call desire is a sentiment whose intensity motivates our behaviour, from the most humdrum and ordinary to the crucial decisions in life.

So here is the problem. A sentiment is by definition something private, something that belongs only to the person who feels it. Only you, the individual who feels that sentiment, can truly know it. If indeed you can, as many of our mental functions belong to the sphere of the unconscious. This idea was first introduced by early theorists of experimental psychology, as well as, of course, by Freud's psychoanalysis.[3] We know now that this idea is fundamentally correct, because psychology and the cognitive neurosciences have supported it with rigorous experimentation. The intrinsic privateness of mental contents appears to deny the possibility of measuring and, consequently, describing how desire shapes behaviour by objective mathematical laws.

And yet, this book tells the story of the idea that made it possible to mathematise desire. It is a strange and intriguing story that begins with a few facts reported by the German physiologist Ernst Heinrich Weber in the first half of the nineteenth century. In the following decades, those facts were to become the foundation of a cultural project known as "psychophysics". The project was given its name by another medical researcher, Gustav Theodor Fechner, who used Weber's observations to establish an empirical science of sensations. Fechner showed how one could measure apparently unobservable and intrinsically private mental states in the laboratory. Yet, while in empirical terms Fechner started from Weber's observations, in theoretical terms his approach had much deeper roots. Indeed, Fechner aimed not to understand what sensations are, but rather to understand the functional relations between sensations and the physical stimuli that trigger them. In other words, Fechner replaced the question "what is...?" with the question "how does it happen that...?".

This replacement is characteristic of the revolution which, from the sixteenth century onwards, abandoned the Aristotelian vision dictating that natural philosophy should seek to investigate essences, that is, to understand the ultimate fundamental reality of things. In the words of one of the founders of modern science, Galileo Galilei:[4] "either we want to attempt to penetrate the true and intrinsic essence of natural substances by investigation, or we accept to remain content to learn about some of the factors that affect them. To investigate the essence, I take it to be an impossible endeavour, an endeavour that is equally fruitless with regard to the elementary substances that are near us and with regard to those that are far away in the skies". Ultimately, this change of perspective allowed Fechner to establish psychophysics on the basis of Weber's observations.[5]

Psychophysics is mostly unknown to anyone who has not studied it at university, yet it underlies the birth of scientific psychology and of contemporary cognitive neuroscience, as well as many technologies that characterise our contemporary world. The conceptual path leading from the measuring of sensations to the empirical study of desire is, however, far from linear. In fact, Fechner's ideas were in a sense anticipated by over a century by the Swiss mathematician Daniel Bernoulli, with reference to what would later be known as "utility" in economics. In psychophysics, the problem of measuring sensations is therefore entwined with that of measuring the motivations underlying economic choice. With the development of modern psychophysics in the twentieth century, new conceptual tools became available for studying decisions and choice behaviour, leading ultimately also to the development of the psychological theory which won the Israeli-American psychologist Daniel Kahneman[6] the 2002 Nobel Prize in Economic Sciences.

As Kahneman himself wrote, his ideas were inspired in many ways by those of Weber and Fechner in psychology, and those of Bernoulli in economics. Kahneman also stated that some of the most important innovations made to his theory of decision-making derive from ideas developed in the field of modern psychophysics. Today, these innovations are applied not only to measuring sensations, but also to analysing a wide range of choice behaviours, in product purchasing, politics, social interaction, in the health field, and even in the sexual sphere. Therefore, after an initial change that represented it in the form of a psychophysical law of sensation, with Kahneman's theory, Weber's intuition became an authentic law of desire.

This is the story I have tried to tell here: a fundamental aspect of our mental life, described in the nineteenth century by a little-known physiologist who was studying something completely different, but in fact anticipated in disguise by a famous Swiss mathematician a century earlier. A theoretical and methodological framework underlying the birth of scientific psychology and of cognitive neuroscience. The idea that inspired a new theory of how we choose which future perspective we choose to pursue, and which won the psychologist who conceived it the Nobel Prize in Economic Sciences. The history of Weber's Law and of psychophysics, a discipline unknown to most but in fact fundamental for understanding a large part of the contemporary world.

Before we begin, one caveat. Psychophysics is a highly technical, formal endeavour. In writing the book, however, I have sought to present a conceptual history of the field, not a scholarly handbook. With this in mind, I have taken a hybrid approach. On the one hand, I have tried to be as accurate as possible in the science, including some mathematical underpinnings, and have followed academic standards for references and notes. On the other hand, I have tried to organise the book and write it to make it not only informative for academic readers, but also engaging for the educated general public. This forced me to take a few shortcuts, ignore some complications, and make some choices. Readers interested in delving into some of the more technical issues are nonetheless directed to relevant references provided in the endnotes. If I managed to strike the right balance is for the reader to judge.

Notes

1. *La ley del deseo* (1987) is a film written, directed, and produced by the Spanish director Pedro Almodovar. It was his sixth film and his first international success.
2. Metonymy is a widely used figure of speech—most likely, you use it all the time. The idea is that we can substitute a noun with the name of something else which is somehow associated to that noun. Examples include substituting something contained with its container ("to eat a dish"—you eat the food, not the dish that contains it), the product of using a tool with the tool itself ("the pen is mightier than the sword"—written language, not the pen, can have longer lasting consequences than violence) or an object with its symbol ("honour the flag"—we honour our country, not the flag that represents it). Interestingly, in Lacan's definition the metonymic substitution refers to the absence of the desired object ("lack of being"), rather than the desired object itself. Desire is thus distinguished from the mere need of the object, fostering an urge to investigate the relationship between the self and the world, in a tension that is both frustrating and satisfying.

3. It is commonly believed that the notion of the unconscious originated with Freud. In fact, the idea was already present in the theorising of philosophers such as Herbart and, most notably, in the work of one of the protagonists of this book, Gustav Theodor Fechner. That of the relationship between the psychoanalyst's and the experimental psychologist's notions of the unconscious is a fascinating problem, but in this book I have chosen to set it aside. For more details, see Romand, D. (2012). Fechner as a pioneering theorist of unconscious cognition. *Consciousness and Cognition*, 21, 562-572.
4. The passage is taken from the Galileo Galilei's third letter to Mark Welser on sunspots (*Villa delle Selve*, 1 December 1612). The full text (in Italian) is available online, e.g.,: https://www.liberliber.it/online/autori/autori-g/galileo-galilei/istoria-e-dimostrazioni-intorno-alle-macchie-solari-e-loro-accidenti-comprese-in-tre-lettere-scritte-allillustrissimo-signor-marco-velseri-linceo/. The translation is mine.
5. This point will need further discussion in the next chapter. In his writings, Fechner explicitly recognised his debt to Weber, who was one of his teachers. However, at least mathematically, what I will here call the Fechner's Law is not necessarily a derivation of Weber's earlier observations.
6. Born in 1934, Kahneman passed in March 2024, while the English version of this book was being finalised. Kahneman would certainly have shared the Nobel Prize with the researcher with whom he worked for many years on this theory, Amos Tversky, had the latter not died prematurely (Nobel Prizes are not awarded posthumously). The Prize motivation was "for having integrated insights from psychological research into economic science, especially concerning human judgment and decision-making under uncertainty".

CHAPTER 2

The Marriage of Heaven and Hell

Abstract "Classical" psychophysics originated with the work of Fechner, which in turn was inspired by Weber's observations, and evolved into more modern approaches in the second half of the last century. In this chapter I tell the story of these developments, which contributed to the foundation of scientific psychology, provided techniques for a variety of sensory-related technologies, and paved the way for unexpected applications to domains such as the measurement of happiness, pain, and choices.

Keywords Psychophysical function • Weber's Law • Fechner's Law • Stevens's Law • Differential threshold • Just-noticeable difference • Absolute threshold

I like to think of the beginning of our story as a set of events that led to a marriage. More precisely, to a conceptual marriage. Of course, the protagonists of this story didn't think of it in these terms. But, at least in the world of ideas, a marriage it was. The marriage was celebrated in 1879, at the University of Leipzig, where Wilhelm Wundt set up the first laboratory of what was then a new discipline. Wundt called it *physiological psychology*.

In the second half of the nineteenth century, European and US researchers began to adapt the methods of the natural sciences to study the mind. Psychology embraced experimentation and abandoned philosophical speculation. For this reason, in university textbooks, 1879 is often mentioned as the birth year of scientific psychology. However, with a dash of poetic license we might say that 1879 was when the English poet and printmaker William Blake, author of the visionary book *The Marriage of Heaven and Hell*, saw his dream come true.

Critical of mystics in the late eighteenth century,[1] Blake rejected the contraposition of spiritual and material, proposing that mind and matter are in fact complementary aspects of the same reality. In the second half of the nineteenth century, the study of this complementarity was made possible in Leipzig, Germany, by a chance encounter followed by a long courtship. This encounter took place in a physiology laboratory, while the courtship continued in the studies and classrooms frequented by a professor, part physicist and part philosopher, ending in the marriage. It was a fruitful marriage, producing an extended family of technologies, applications, experimental paradigms, and measuring methods. As often happens, the marriage also went through a rather itchy patch, but it survived, enriched by a greater awareness of its own foundations.

A Chance Encounter

Ernst Heinrich Weber was a professor and researcher who worked in Leipzig in the first half of the nineteenth century.[2] A relatively unknown scientific figure, his works investigated various aspects of physiology and anatomy. He researched the neurophysiological bases of touch, the hydrodynamics of blood circulation, the effect of delivering electrical stimulation to the brain on the autonomic nervous system. He also discovered the apparatus (*Weber's ossicles*) that links the swim bladder with the inner ear in some fish species, the function of which is still being studied today. Many of his works investigated the neural structures involved in tactile perception,[3] which Weber studied by gathering information on the sensory responses caused by stimuli administered to different parts of the body.

One of the things Weber observed was that the distance perceived by touch between two pressure points depends on the area on which they are applied. Imagine a compass, the two points set apart at a distance of 1 cm. If you close your eyes and press the two points firstly on the palm of your hand and then on the inner forearm, the two points will seem further apart on the hand. If you then press them on your stomach, you will probably feel only one pressure point rather than two. Weber hypothesised that this phenomenon was caused by the distribution of the nerve endings beneath the skin, which are denser in some areas (palm), less dense in others (forearm), and even less dense elsewhere (stomach). This hypothesis was later confirmed in the second half of the nineteenth century, when other researchers discovered the mechanical receptors in the skin, muscles, and bowel. Today we know that variations in the density of skin receptors correspond to variations in the area of the cortical area that receives their signals.[4]

But while gathering these data, Weber also realised something else: the more intense the pressure stimuli, the less able we are to discriminate between them. Imagine doing an experiment (if you are so inclined, you may even wish to actually do it—but bear in mind that the numbers below have been slightly adjusted for the sake of simplicity). Hold a box containing 100 nails, each weighing 1 gram, in your right hand. Hold another box in your left hand, containing, let's say, 101. Try to weigh them. Can you decide which is the heavier? Perhaps, but it is more likely that you can't. Then try with 102 nails. Now you may notice the difference. It would therefore seem that the ability to discriminate between two weights requires an increase of 2 grams. This is, however, valid when the starting weight is 100 grams. Now imagine placing 1000 nails in the two boxes. If you add 2 more to the box in your left hand, you won't feel any difference. Now you would have to add around 20. With a starting weight of 100 grams you can detect a change of about 2 grams, whereas with a starting weight of 1000 grams you can't, you will need an increase of about 20 grams. The rule therefore seems to be that the ability to discriminate is proportional to the starting weight. In fact, the discriminable increment increases in absolute terms (in the example, from 2 to 20 grams), but remains constant in relation to the starting weight (in our example, this is always around 2%).

Weber devoted only a few words to this observation in some passages of his works. However, that observation was destined to become a general principle for measuring sensations, applied to many other fields, including the measurement of the perceived intensity of a sound, the perceived luminosity of the stars, and the perceived numerosity of a set of elements. This principle is known as "Weber's Law". However, it was not named in this way by Weber but by Gustav Theodor Fechner, another researcher working at the University of Leipzig. Because of Fechner, today we write Weber's Law using this formula:

$$\Delta I / I = k$$

which states that two physical quantities, ΔI and I, are in a constant relationship k. To understand its meaning for the problem of desire, we must, however, specify two things. The first concerns the quantity indicated by I, which does not refer to the intensity of any physical energy but to the intensity of a form of energy able to stimulate an organism's perceptual system. As even those who have never studied psychology know, one fundamental mental function is to acquire information on the objects and events populating the environment we live in. Psychologists and neuroscientists call this function *perception*. What makes perception possible is a fact of physics: there must be energy in the environment to stimulate the nerve cells that are able to transform energy into a neural signal. There are different types of these cells in human perceptual systems. Each of them is specific to one of three forms of energy: electromagnetic (light), mechanical, and chemical. The complex process which, in the brain, enables us to see, hear, touch, taste, and smell starts with one of these forms of energy.

The second issue to be clarified concerns the meaning of ΔI. This refers to the threshold, i.e., the minimum increase in intensity that enables us to perceive a difference in comparison to an initial intensity I.[5] Weber's Law states that the ratio between the threshold ΔI and the intensity I is constant. This means that the threshold is directly proportional to the initial intensity. If we multiply the terms to the left and right of the equal sign by I, the equivalence remains true, and given that $I/I = 1$, $\Delta I/I = k$ becomes $\Delta I = kI$, which is like saying that the threshold becomes bigger and bigger as the initial intensity increases. We saw an example of this phenomenon in our imaginary experiment on weight discrimination. Another example of the same principle, referring to the visual perception of numerosity, is given in Fig. 2.1.

But, you may object, all this seems to concern the physical world and not the mind. After all, a physical quantity is something objective, that we can measure—in the case of weight, for example, with scales. But consider the imaginary experiment described above. We imagined testing one's tested ability to discriminate between pairs of stimuli. This is a mental faculty, something that your perceptual mind does, and that could make you conscious of a difference (or not). Of course, nobody can observe the contents of your consciousness. They are yours, and nobody else's. But thresholds are not. Thresholds are public, and we can measure them as physical changes in intensity. In our example, we can put the stimuli on scales and record differences in weight. However, thresholds are also an indirect measurement of mental faculty. A low threshold is the hallmark of

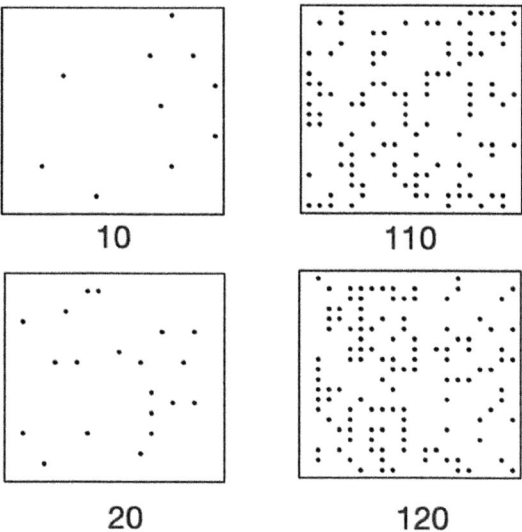

Fig. 2.1 Four squares containing 10, 20, 110, and 120 dots. The difference between 20 and 10 dots is equal to the difference between 110 and 120. But in the first case, there clearly seems to be more dots in the lower square than in the upper square. In the second case, on the other hand, there seems to be the same number in each square. In the first case, therefore, the increase of 10 dots allows us to notice the difference, while in the second case a larger increase would be necessary. This is precisely Weber's Law. *Source*: Wikimedia Commons CC BY-SA 4.0 (image in the public domain)

good discrimination—we can tell relatively small differences apart. Conversely, a high threshold implies poor discrimination, as we need greater differences to notice that something has changed. And here's the thing: by measuring the physical change in threshold, it becomes indirectly possible to measure a corresponding psychological change, the change in one's ability to discriminate. In this way, Weber's Law becomes a tool for studying the complementarity of the world of physics and the world of psychology; objective and subjective; mind and matter. A simple idea, yet destined to become an ambitious project, that of mathematising the functional relationship between the physical stimuli in the environment and their effects on the mental processes of an organism.

The Long Courtship

We mentioned that Weber himself did not understand the importance of "his" law. It was Fechner, another researcher working at the University of Leipzig, who coined the term "Weber's Law", noticing that what for Weber was a marginal observation could become the ingredient of a successful marriage. Despite also having a medical background, Fechner's interests were much broader than Weber's. Soon after graduating, under the pseudonym Doctor Mises, he even published a treatise entitled *Anatomie der Engel* ("The Comparative Anatomy of Angels"), a kind of theological and metaphysical parody that ironically tackled questions such as the shape of angels, their functions, and, of course, that age-old problem of their sex.

However, due to the variety of his interests and for health reasons, Fechner's academic career was far less linear than Weber's. He enrolled in Medicine in 1817, the same year in which Weber obtained his first teaching post, but after graduating in 1822, he began to study mathematics and physics, and in 1834 became a professor of Physics. Due to serious neurological problems, in 1840 he was forced to leave teaching for a while. On his return, Fechner had become a kind of scientist-philosopher. The topics of his lessons ran from natural philosophy to the relationship between the mind and body, psychology, and aesthetics. Fechner was therefore exposed to Weber's ideas, both as a student and as a colleague, and his interests placed him in the ideal position to gradually understand their theoretical implications. This courtship lasted for two more decades, until the publication, in 1860, of *Elemente der Psychophysik* ("Elements of Psychophysics"). He defined this new discipline, psychophysics, as the "precise doctrine of the functional relationships or dependence between the body and soul or, more generally, between the bodily world and the spiritual world, between the physical and the psychical".

Today we would say Fechner sought to identify a "law of sensations". In other words, he sought to build a mathematical model that could describe how mental contents change when one changes physical quantities. To build this model, Fechner started from the empirical data of Weber's Law, although he proposed a different interpretation. For Weber the increase ΔI refers to the threshold, but Fechner interpreted it as an infinitesimal—arbitrarily small—increase in a physical stimulus I, to which it is possible to associate a corresponding infinitesimal increase in a psychological quantity s, the sensation. Fechner understood that the constant

k in Weber's Law can be interpreted as a measure of the subjective change of a sensation, when the quantity ΔI is added to I.

Said in a more concise yet more technical manner, Fechner rewrote Weber's Law as a differential equation:

$$ds = c \cdot dI / I$$

where dI is the infinitesimal increase in physical intensity, ds the corresponding infinitesimal increase in the sensation, I the intensity in relation to which we calculate dI. The symbol · indicates a multiplication, and c is a constant of proportionality. Using differential calculus and algebra, Fechner obtained what is known today as "Fechner's Law".[6]

According to Fechner's Law, sensation s, measured in psychological units, is proportional to the logarithm of the ratio between I and an initial intensity I_0. In symbols, it is written as follows:[7]

$$s = c \cdot \log(I / I_0)$$

The formula for Fechner's Law is relatively straightforward, but there is a potential problem. At least in my experience, even among people with a university degree there are some who have never learnt, or have forgotten, what a logarithm is. If you are one of those, don't lose heart. The logarithm of number x, log (x), is the exponent to which another number, known as the *base*, must be raised to obtain x. The base can be any number, but 10 is often used. Thus, the logarithm in base 10 of 10 is 1, because 10 raised to the first power is equal to 10. The logarithm in base 10 of 100 is 2, because 10 raised to the second power is equal to 100. And so on: log 10 (1,000) = 3, log 10 (10,000) = 4, log 10 (100,000) = 5, etc. The logarithm in any base of 1 is zero.

Note that, in the example, the logarithm in base 10 represents the number of zeros following the first digit. This is rather like saying that the logarithm in base 10 represents an "order of magnitude" i.e., if we are working in the hundreds, or the thousands, etc. One consequence of this is that the logarithmic function is a curve with a characteristic concave shape, in which the quantity on the y-axis rises sharply at the beginning, when the quantity on the x-axis is small, but then starts to grow evermore slowly until it stops growing entirely when the quantity on the x-axis is equal to infinite.

To a mathematician, it is perfectly reasonable for a quantity to reach an infinite value. In practice, of course, we never reach infinity, but when a quantity on the *y*-axis becomes very large, the growth of the curve is so slow that it becomes negligible. It is as if the curve had flattened out completely. This is shown in Fig. 2.2.

Let's take a look at the figure. To draw a graph like this, I had to choose a value for the constant *k* of Weber's Law as well as a range of values for *I*. The first is usually measured in the laboratory, studying the discrimination capacity in the relevant conditions. For the second, I chose values which should be fairly realistic, in certain conditions, when a person holds an object that is not too heavy in their hand. Given that this is above all for illustration purposes, I also chose values for which it is easy to note the fundamental characteristic of a logarithmic function.

As we can see in the figure, a logarithmic curve is a curve in which equal differences on the *y*-axis (in our case, sensation) correspond to equal ratios on the *x*-axis (the physical units of weight). For instance, the difference in sensation (the distance on the *y*-axis) is the same between 3 and 4 and between 5 and 6. However, these distances do not correspond to equal

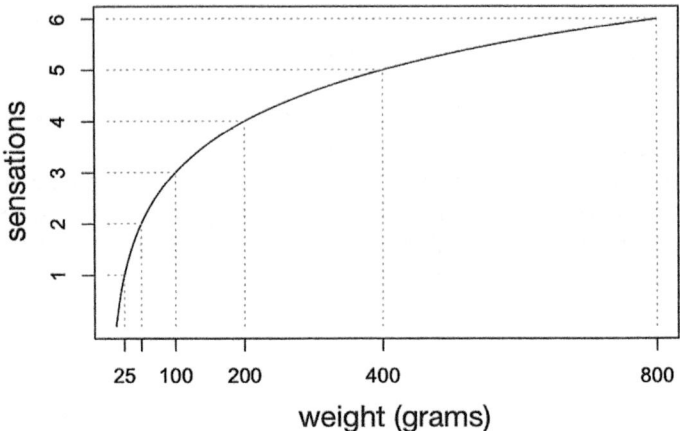

Fig. 2.2 Fechner's Law for the sensation of weight, assuming that Weber's constant ratio between threshold and intensity is equal to 0.05 and that the absolute threshold is equal to 12.5 grams. The "units of sensation" on the *y*-axis are arbitrary. Note that equal ratios between weights on the *x*-axis correspond to equal differences in sensations on the *y*-axis

distances on the x axis, but rather equal ratios. In the first case, the distance x is 200-100 = 100 grams, while in the second it is 800-400 = 400 grams. The ratio 200/100 on the other hand remains equal to the ratio 800/400 (always 2:1). Consequently, as the weight increases, increasingly large increments are required to produce equal effects on sensation, which is, once again, the fundamental concept expressed by Weber's Law.[8]

Finally, it will not have escaped careful readers of the first part of this paragraph that, to build the graph in the figure, I had to set a value for I_0. This aspect is quite important, as it corresponds to a typical assumption of "classic" Fechnerian psychophysics, i.e., that it is possible to set a value I for which sensation is zero. This value is called the *absolute threshold*. For many types of sensation, there are methods that can be used to measure thresholds with a good degree of approximation. In these cases, Fechner's Law is a very useful model, as we will see shortly.

Having said this, it should also be specified that modern psychophysics has increasingly problematised the concept of threshold, in both theoretical and empirical terms. It has also developed approaches to Fechner's problem that dispense with thresholds completely. These approaches, described in the next chapter, played an important role in transforming Fechner's Law of sensation into an authentic law of desire. But before tackling this issue, we should meet some members of the extended family that grew gradually during the marriage.

An Extended Family

Following the publication of *Elements,* psychophysics developed in several directions, partly due to practical issues. Any apparatus that acts as an interface between a mechanical—or electronic—system and a human operator requires the exchange of information between human and machine, and these interactions obey psychophysical laws. Today, we all carry these interfaces around in our pockets: they are in our mobile phone, watch, tablet. Yet the precursors of these systems made their appearance between the late nineteenth and early twentieth century. Just think of the cinema and the radio. All these things worked because a system modulates a form of energy in time and space, stimulating the perceptual systems of a user who obtains information from them. We have to take psychophysics into account when designing these things, and Fechner's Law found (and still finds today) direct applications in acoustics, lighting, the design of television screens, computers, and mobile phones.

Consider your experience of sounds. When we hear sounds, we hear that they are long or short, high-pitched or low-pitched, and most importantly weak and hardly audible—like the wind rustling through tree leaves—or loud and almost deafening, like a pneumatic drill on a building site. A very well-known unit of measurement for the intensity of a sound sensation is the *decibel*. For instance, standing at a distance of one metre, rustling leaves have a perceived intensity of around 10 decibels, and the pneumatic drill around 100 decibels. Developed in the 1920s in the Bell Telephone laboratories, the decibel unit of measurement can be defined as

$$dB = c \cdot \log(P/P_0)$$

where *dB* stands for decibel, *P* is a physical measure of the mechanical energy of the vibration emitted from a sound source, and P_0 is the value of energy corresponding to the zero sensation.

The decibel scale is therefore none other than the Weber-Fechner Law for the sensation of sound intensity, with the constant *c* that depends on how the energy is measured. The decibel scale is useful for solving many practical problems. It can help to prevent deafness: prolonged exposure to sounds above 90 decibels causes partial hearing loss, and sounds exceeding 120–140 decibels can cause permanent damage. If you have to use a pneumatic drill for a long time, wear hearing protectors!

Another example is how we change the "volume" of the output sound of a music playing device, CD- or record-player, but also a television, computer, or smartphone. The device will have some kind of control mechanism, a dial to turn or a button to press. But how is this mechanism designed? Given that the sensation of sound intensity obeys Fechner's Law, the effect of increasing sound energy varies depending on where we start. When the energy is low (starting from a weak sound), the tiniest increase will produce a considerable change in perceived intensity. Conversely, when the energy is high (starting from a loud sound), the very same increase will remain undetected. For this reason, the dial mechanism must be calibrated to take into account the psychophysical relationship between decibel and sound energy. An equal movement will produce increasing physical changes, corresponding to equal changes in the sensation, in accordance with the law.

Fechner's Law measures the perceived intensity of a sound with excellent approximation. However, the problem of measuring the sensation of intensity is even more interesting, because, as anyone who has studied a little music will know, a sound also varies in frequency. The frequency of vibration is the physical basis for the sensation of pitch. For instance, the rumble of thunder in the distance is a deep, low-frequency sound, while a chirping bird is a bright, high-frequency sound. In the same way, the note "A" in the central octave of a piano keyboard corresponds to a frequency of 440 Hertz, while the same note on the next octave up has a frequency of 880 Hertz, the next octave up again above 1760 Hertz, and so on. They are all the same note, but we perceive them as increasingly high in pitch.

Now, the perceived dimension that runs from high- to low-pitched seems to be something completely different from the dimension that runs from soft to loud. It is one thing to play the same "A" *pianissimo* or *fortissimo*; it is another thing to play two notes in different octaves with the same intensity. Or at least that's how it seems; but that's not exactly how it is, because the sensation of how intense a sound is in fact depends also on its frequency. For instance, a sound with low physical intensity is generally still audible if its frequency lies in the range between 400 and 4000 Hz (approximately, the most prominent frequencies in the human voice), but the same level of intensity can become imperceivable if the sound frequency is above 4000–5000 Hz, and will certainly be entirely imperceivable if it has a frequency of less than 400 Hz. The definition given above of the decibel is therefore only valid if we specify the frequency at which the sound is measured.[9]

One solution to the problem involves using not the value P0, which measures the energy corresponding to the zero sensation for a sound at a specific frequency, but rather a common agreed upon reference intensity. This level is indicated by the acronym SPL (sound pressure level). When using the SPL, the Weber-Fechner Law for sound intensity becomes

$$dB_{SPL} = c \cdot \log(P / SPL)$$

which is similar to the previous formula but measures the perceived intensity on the same scale also for sounds with different frequencies.

The SPL decibel scale offers an excellent approximation of the perceived intensity of a physical sound, at least when this consists of vibrations at well-defined frequencies and under controlled conditions. One example of this is the audiometric tests performed in a clinic to assess hearing loss, using earphones. Another application, in music reproduction, is the "loudness" button we find in many stereo system amplifiers. When we press this button, the low frequency components, and to a certain extent also the high frequency components, of a complex sound are emphasised to compensate the lower sensitivity compared to intermediate frequencies. This is useful when listening to music at low volume, enhancing sounds that would otherwise be hard to perceive. In this way, when we listen to a symphony at low volume, we can hear the double-bass along with the violins.

Another example is sound level meters used to assess noise pollution. These instruments have a circuit that corrects the signal so that the response of the instrument reproduces that of the auditory system (a "weighting" circuit). Sound meters do not, however, guarantee a precise measurement when the sounds have many different frequencies, as many natural and artificial noises do. This problem is partly resolved using different weighting circuits to suit the conditions. For instance, there is a specific weighting to assess the noise level of air traffic. It should also be said that this approach to measuring the sensation of intensity does not consider any effects caused by the context, such as the presentation of other sounds immediately before the sound being assessed.

Similar considerations can also be made in relation to the problem of measuring the perceived intensity of light, which had already been investigated by the first astronomers in history. Hipparchus, who lived in Greece around 2200 years ago, is considered to be the greatest astronomer of ancient times. He is attributed with the first attempt to classify stars into classes of "magnitude". Hipparchus identified six different magnitudes, corresponding to stars that appeared to him as equal increments in apparent intensity. In the nineteenth century, when instruments to measure physical intensity became available, it became apparent that Hipparchu's magnitudes approximately corresponded to constant ratios between intensity levels. In the second half of the nineteenth century, Robert Pogson, a young researcher working at the Radcliffe Observatory in Oxford, realised that Hipparchus's observations were consistent with Fechner's Law.[10] Pogson therefore proposed to consider the energy emitted by the brightest stars (first magnitude) equal to 100, setting the ratio in the progression of light energy at the fifth root of 100, which is (approximating to the second decimal place) 2.51.

In this way, on the 1-to-6 scale of magnitudes, he made energy correspond to $2.51^5 = 100$, $2.51^4 = 39,818$, and so on up to $2.51^1 = 2.51$ and finally $2.51^0 = 1$. Using this "Pogson's Law", which once again is pretty much the same thing as Fechner's Law, it later became possible to attribute magnitudes even to stars that are not visible to the naked eye, but only through a telescope, extending the scale to very weak intensities. Using telescopes placed on satellites or space probes, today we can observe stars of magnitudes up to 30, far less intense than Hipparchus's lower limit. It is also possible to attribute a magnitude of less than 1 or even a negative magnitude to stars with apparent magnitudes that were previously grouped together in the first category.

For instance, Sirius, the brightest star in the sky, has a magnitude of -1.46. This also allows us to extend the scale to stars that were originally excluded from the classification, those that do not appear as light spots, like the sun (which has a magnitude of -26.7) and the moon (magnitude -12.7). Note that in these cases, the negative does not mean the absence or reduction of light but rather an increase. I strongly suspect that this remains a source of confusion for many inexperienced students and readers of textbooks on the subject. Naturally, the historical origins of this fact lie in Hipparchus's classification, based on a kind of ranking of the importance of the stars, as well as the use that Pogson made of it.

But I fear we will have to come to terms with this counter-intuitive aspect. The scale of magnitudes plays a consolidated role in astronomic science and is now used to quantify magnitudes that have little to do with measuring the sensation perceived by a person. Worthy of mention, on the other hand, is the fact that in modern astronomy, magnitudes are no longer just a place in a ranking list, but an actual number that can also take on intermediate values between the integers, as in the case of the sun and the moon.

This distinction is not limited to the scale of magnitude: it is generally relevant to the problem of how to interpret a value assigned to the sensation s in Fechner's Law. Also in this case, we can interpret s simply as the position in a kind of league table of gradually more intense discrete sensations arranged in increasing order. Or we may think that s represents a genuine measurement of the intensity of a sensation. In this case, it would be correct to state, for instance, that a sensation with intensity 4.5 has twice the intensity of a sensation with intensity 2.25. To do this, however, we have to establish a unit of measurement, and set a 'benchmark' physical intensity in which the measurement is equal to zero.

In Fechner's Law, this is done starting from the concept of threshold, reasoning in the following manner. Having determined the value I_0 below which the sensation is zero, I is increased to find the value $I_1 = I_0 + \Delta I_0$ so that the sensation can be distinguished from the previous one. For I_1 we can make s equal to a *jnd*, or a "just noticeable" difference.[11] Now we can imagine proceeding in the same way, increasing I_1 until we find $I_2 = I_1 + \Delta I_1$, which will be s equal to two *jnds*. And so on. This rationale is equivalent to the one used to measure, for instance, a length. Saying that an object is 1.5 metres long means that, having set a unit of measurement equal to a standard that we call metre, the length of that object is one and a half times the standard.

The idea is that, assuming that all jnds are equal in sensation regardless of the reference intensity, it should be possible to use the jnd as the unit of measurement of the psychological dimension. Therefore, for instance, if the sensation s caused by an intensity I is equal to 1.5 jnds, its perceived intensity is equal to one and a half times the benchmark sensation, namely, 1 jnd. All this is, however, possible only if we can measure the thresholds needed to count the jnds. In particular, it must be possible to set the absolute threshold, the starting point in which the sensation is zero. In fact, from Fechner onwards, psychophysics developed numerous methods for measuring thresholds. However, research in this field has also clarified that the very concept of sensory threshold is far less obvious than it might seem at first glance, and that only in well-defined cases can it be put into practice. The matter therefore becomes quite complicated, but also more interesting. This is why the whole of the following chapter is devoted to deconstructing the concept of threshold. As we shall see, the fundamental intuition implicit in Weber's Law can be incorporated in psychophysical approaches that do away with thresholds completely.

THE SEVENTIETH-YEAR ITCH

Marriages often have their highs and lows, happy times and more difficult periods. Our psychophysical marriage suffered a serious itch more or less around the 1950s. Until then, the Fechner's Law had continued to be confirmed, not only as it worked well to quantify the intensity of sensations in many fields, but also because some physiologists had observed elements of the nervous system that appeared to comply with a logarithmic law. Between the 1920s and '30s, it had in fact become possible to make the first recordings of nerve activity in animal models. For instance, studying neural units in the compound eye of a crustacean, the US physiologist Haldan Keffer Hartline[12] observed that the maximum response frequency increased with the logarithm of light intensity.

In truth, some minor difficulties were noted in the years immediately following the publication of Fechner's *Elemente*. One of these came from experimental studies, because these soon demonstrated that the ratios between ΔI and I were not always constant for all values of I, as Weber's Law stated. In 1924, the physiologist Selig Hecht[13] published an article documenting how, in the perception of brightness, Weber's Law describes data well only in a range of intermediate intensities. When the light intensity is very low or very high, Weber's Law describes the data only very approximately. The data produced by the physiologists were also far from definitive. For instance, Hartline's results seemed consistent with Weber when taking into consideration the peak of neural response, but not when analysing other characteristics of the evolution of the response over time. Around the 1950s, the itch became even stronger, with the introduction of new methods by one of the most important methodologists of scientific psychology, the American Stanley Smith Stevens.[14]

Stevens research problem was the same as Fechner's. He sought to identify the mathematical law that describes the functional relationship between the physical and the psychical. However, in contrast to Fechner, Stevens did not start from Weber's Law and the study of thresholds, but from empirical data collected using a method he called *magnitude estimation*. Stevens had begun his career in the field of psychoacoustics and was interested in identifying efficient methods for measuring auditory sensations. He came up with an idea: given that we are interested in measuring sensation, and the person who has access to the sensation is the person who feels it, why not simply ask the person to tell us?

Imagine the situation. At the beginning of an experimental session, you are presented with a randomly chosen tone and asked to represent the intensity of that tone with a number. You are also told that this sound must be used as a reference for the following tones. At this point, you are presented with all the other tones, in random order. For each one, you must simply repeat what you did with the first one, making sure that the chosen number reflects sensation intensity in relation to the initial reference. In this way, if you assigned the number 10 to the first reference, and then you hear a tone that seems to you to be twice as intense, you have to say 20. If it seems half as intense, you have to say 5, and so on.

The experiment is repeated with a few dozen participants, then calculating the averages of the individual estimates for each presented tone. Using these experimentally calculated averages, it is possible to build a mathematical model of how magnitude estimations increase with intensity, and this model is a psychophysical function. Stevens conducted many experiments like this, examining dozens of different types of sensation, from sound intensity to vibration, to the brightness of a spot or disc in a fixed area, to the length of a segment, the area of a surface, the intensity of a taste, the sensation of hot or cold, pressure on the palm of the hand, the roughness of a material, the intensity of an electric shock. For each of these sensations, the function is a curve, which in some cases resembles the Fechner curve. In other cases, it is significantly different from the Fechner curve. However, all the curves are described by the function

$$s = c \cdot I^a$$

where a is an exponent specific to the sensation under consideration, and c is now a constant that depends on the unit of measurement, which we can ignore. Figure 2.3, left, shows three examples. The function for the intensity of a sound sensation has an exponent of 0.33 and is a curve which is not so different in shape from the Fechner curve. The function of the intensity of an electric shock has an exponent greater than 1 (approximately 3.5), which makes it very different from the Fechner curve. The "curve" relating to the sensation of a length for a segment, shown in grey, has an exponent of almost exactly 1, and therefore the function becomes $y = x$, a straight line.

In 1957, Stevens published a widely cited article[15] in the prestigious journal "Psychological Review". In that paper, he asserted that a general rule of the functional relationship between sensations and physical stimuli does exist, but it is not Fechner's Law. For Stevens, the real general law is in fact that in which "equal *ratios* between physical stimuli correspond to equal *ratios* between subjective sensations".[16] This is in fact a major difference between the two psychophysical functions. In Fechner's log function, the functional relationship between sensations and stimuli envisages that an arithmetic progression in sensations corresponds to a geometric progression in the stimuli. An arithmetic progression is a succession of numbers in which the difference between each term and the following term is kept constant. This is exactly what happens in Fechner's logarithmic law: equal increases in sensation correspond to equal ratios in physical intensity. A geometric progression, on the other hand, is a succession of numbers in which the ratio between each term and the following term is kept constant. This is what happens in Stevens's power law: equal ratios in the stimulus correspond to equal ratios in the sensation.

To convince you of this, take a ruler and examine in detail one of the curves in Fig. 2.3, for example, the one with exponent 0.33. The physical intensities (x-axis) 20 and 40 have a ratio of 1 to 2 (40 is two times 20). The corresponding intensities of sensation are (approximating to the nearest decimal) 26.9 and 33.8, which have a ratio of 4 to 5 (again approximating to the nearest decimal). The distance between the physical intensities 40 and 80 corresponds again to the ratio 2 to 1, and the corresponding intensities of sensation 33.8 and 42.5 still have a ratio of 4 to 5. And so on. For this reason, Stevens's function becomes a straight line if the quantity on the x-axis and y-axis on the graph are both subjected to a log transformation. Figure 2.3, right, shows the effects of the transformation on the curves on the left. Thus, Stevens's Law can also be written as:

$$\log(s) = \log(c) + a \cdot \log(I)$$

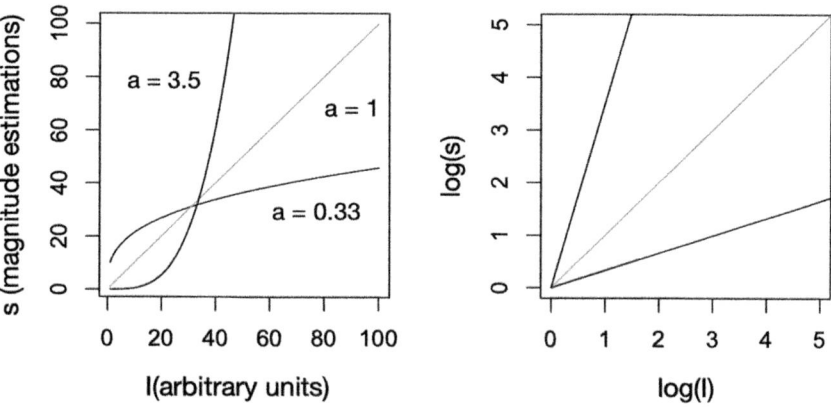

Fig. 2.3 Left: Psychophysical functions for the sensations of sound intensity (exponent 0.33), visual length of a segment (straight line in grey, exponent 1), and intensity of an electric shock (exponent 3.5), according to Stevens. The curves are drawn assuming that I is measured in the same arbitrary units. Right: the same functions redrawn after the log transformation of both axes. The slopes of the three lines correspond to the exponents of the original functions

where the slope of the line, that is, the constant a for which log (I) must be multiplied to obtain (s), is the exponent of the corresponding curve. This interpretation of Stevens's Law will prove useful for us shortly.

Another major difference between Fechner's Law and Stevens's Law is that the latter mathematically represents a family of curves, which have different characteristics. As in the case of the sensation of sound intensity shown in Fig. 2.4, in some of these the sensation grows rapidly at the start, and then gradually less so as x increases. These curves are therefore "negatively accelerated" or "compressive" (Steven's favourite term) as also occurs in Fechner's Law. So, the Fechner and Stevens curves resemble each other, even though, to be precise, if we overlaid them we would see that they are close only in a rather narrow area of the graph. In other cases, like the electric shock, Stevens's curve grows slowly at the beginning, then rises sharply. This type of curve is "positively accelerated", or "expansive", and it has a completely different trend in comparison to that of a logarithmic curve.

The rule is that with exponents of less than 1, the curve is negatively accelerated; with exponents of more than 1, they are positively accelerated. Stevens recorded negative exponents for sensations like sound intensity, vibration, brightness, the area of a surface; and positive exponents for sensations like electric shock, salty tastes, and cold on the body. Interpreting differences between different exponents is not always crystal clear, also because their value depends on the specific characteristics of the administered stimulus. For instance, Stevens recorded an exponent of 1.6 for heat administered through contact with a metallic object, 1.3 for heat administered through radiation of a small portion of skin, but 0.7 for heat administered by radiation of the whole body.

What is certain, and relevant to the interpretation of the mathematics, is that a psychophysical curve with negative acceleration tends to compress

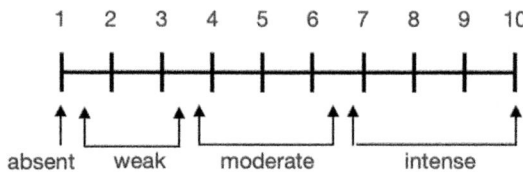

Fig. 2.4 The magnitude estimation method applied to measuring pain. The patient is asked to mark the intensity of the sensation on a scale of 1–10

the response in relation to the input physical intensity. This means that sensitivity can extend to a very wide range of intensities, from very weak to very intense. The reasoning behind this is more or less as follows: if the stimulus is weak, it is advantageous for an organism to be sensitive to minute changes in the input signal; if, on the other hand, it is very intense, a minor change has little impact on behaviour. To optimise the ability of an organism to interact with its environment, therefore, it clearly makes sense for the sensory system in this case to have a negatively accelerated response. In our environment, we take advantage of information contained in light or sound vibrations in a very wide range of intensities. For instance, a visual system that works in both bright light and shadow and an auditory system that responds to both very weak and very intense sounds are very useful. Not by chance, many forms of visual and auditory sensation have curves with exponents of less than 1. With a curve with positive acceleration, on the other hand, the response is expanded in relation to the input intensity. If we touch an electric wire, there is no benefit in perceiving the intensity of the shock even when the current is very intense. If anything, we should stop the potentially hazardous stimulus. With these types of stimuli, it is therefore reasonable for the response to have a positive acceleration. In the same way, a moderately expansive curve will optimise the response to stimuli which are not necessarily harmful but which are significant for an organism only in a relatively narrow range of intensities. This is valid, for example, for the concentration of certain substances in foods or perfumes.

For all these reasons, Stevens thought that the power function offered a measure of sensation that was not only more useful but also more consistent with empirical data. There was clearly a crisis. Fechner hoped to identify a truly general law, but Stevens's methods actually offered broader possibilities for application than methods that involved time-consuming procedures. In practice, Stevens's psychophysics began to be used in many different fields, including the psychophysics of smell and taste, among others. One of the most commonly used methods for quantifying pain in clinical fields consists in presenting a numerical scale, usually accompanied by verbal labels, and asking the patient to mark the level of the pain sensation with a pen (Fig. 2.4). This of course is none other than the magnitude estimation method invented by Stevens. The method used in computer graphics to calibrate the intensity of the screen in order to obtain the broadest possible range of colours is also based on a power function. In the same way, Fechner's psychophysics continued to be used in fields such as sound measurement, although Stevens had proposed an alternative psychophysical scale to the decibel. Today, the two approaches are still used in both basic research and practical applications.

As we well know, marriages on the rocks often survive for practical reasons. This is more or less the case of our psychophysical marriage. Still today, in scientific literature it is not unusual to find works that use Fechner's methods, as well as works that use Stevens's. In many cases, what matters is to have a measuring procedure that can produce stable and replicable results in subsequent experiments, in order to be able to compare different experimental conditions. If I am interested in studying the effect of certain conditions of stimulation on the sensation of how big an object is, I have to compare measurements taken in those conditions with measurements taken without those conditions. The model used for taking the measurements is not important, as long as it is the same in both cases. One can pick the method that best fits the equipment in use, the time available for collecting the data, and so on. Of course, it is a different matter if we think in terms of applications or in terms of theory. In the latter case, the aim is more ambitious, because we want to understand a regularity observed in a natural phenomenon. If this is the purpose, the deep-down motivations for the itch return to the surface, and the dilemma comes back to the fore: what is the exact shape of the relationship between the physical and the mental? Fechner's Law or Stevens's Law? Modern psychophysics remains divided on this point, but we are beginning to catch a glimpse of one plausible solution. The answer seems to come from computational neuroscience and consists of a compromise.

In the 1960s, some researchers worked on a model that would entail a logarithmic function when the data are threshold measurements, but a power function when they derive from procedures such as magnitude estimation. One fundamental study was published in 1963 by the physicist Donald MacKay, from the Department of Neuroscience at Keele University in the United Kingdom. Without going into detail, the argument proposed by MacKay is based on two assumptions, both of which are plausible. The first is that the sensitivity of a sensory system in an organism is inversely proportional to the intensity of the physical stimulus (this is of course Fechner's Law, however applied to neural activation, which is different from the perceived intensity of sensation). The second is that the emission of a response like an estimation of magnitude or similar by an organism is not based only on the sensory system but also requires other operations. In particular, MacKay suggested that response can be described as an operation that consists in some kind of comparison between the input sensory activation and an internal signal, and that this operation in turn produces a logarithmic response. MacKay therefore proposed that the response of the organism can be described as a log transformation which is the function of another log transformation. This produces a relationship between input signal and response similar to Stevens's Law, in its second formulation described above.

Towards the end of his career, Stevens himself acknowledged that this line of reasoning appears to be correct. Both laws should therefore be valid, in their respective fields of competence. When data merely reflect sensory discrimination, the description offered by Fechner's Law tends to be better. When they reflect a more complex response, Stevens's Law works better. Both models are however incomplete, and works that attempt to unify the two approaches continued to be published.[17] The main development of modern psychophysics has however moved in a different direction, radically changing how we think about thresholds and sensitivity. This has made it possible to extend the measurement of sensations also in relation to stimuli that cannot be described as physical intensities, and ultimately, to desire.

Notes

1. In particular, the Swedish theologian Emanuel Swedenborg, who about 30 years earlier, published a book entitled *Heaven and Hell*, a rather mystic vision of afterlife based on the clear distinction between the spiritual and materials worlds.
2. Weber graduated in Medicine in 1815, the year of the Battle of Waterloo, and obtained his first academic post two years later at the University of Leipzig, where he remained until he retired in 1871.
3. Weber published his first work on the physiology of touch in 1834, in Latin. The book was entitled *De Subtilitate Tactus* ("On the Sense of Touch"). At that time, Latin was losing its role as the international language of science, and ten years later Weber published *Der Tatsinn und das Gemeingefühl* ("The Sense of Touch and the Common Sensibility") in German. Weber used the term "common sensibility" to mean the set of mechanical, visceral, muscular, thermal and pain sensations we feel in the body (for more information on this, see N. Bruno and F. Pavani, *Perception: A Multisensory Perspective*, Oxford, Oxford University Press, 2018.)
4. In the cortical area devoted to touch, parts that receive signals from skin districts with the most receptors are larger than those that receive signals

from less dense districts. For example, the part devoted to the palm of the hand is far larger than that receiving signals from the belly, despite the fact that the palm is much smaller. The cortical "magnification" of some skin districts is one of the factors that contribute to the conscious perception of the objects we touch (but not the only one).

5. Technically, this is the definition of a *differential* threshold, a measure of resolution power. In Fechner's psychophysics, differential thresholds are not to be confused with *absolute* thresholds, which measure the smallest stimulus intensities that cause sensations, in each given sensory domain. The first are usually measured by assessing discrimination between two stimuli, the second by assessing detection of a single, very weak, stimulus. We will return to absolute thresholds in the next chapter.

6. In many texts, this is also called the Weber-Fechner Law, precisely to underline that Fechner used Weber's observation as one of his starting points. However, things are more complicated. Although Fechner did use Weber's Law as a starting point for his derivation of a psychophysical function, later analyses have shown that it is possible to derive Fechner's Law without assuming Weber's. Thus, from a rigorous mathematical standpoint, the two turn out to be independent. Consistent with this conclusion, it has been pointed out that in Fechner's work there is a second derivation which did not use Weber's, and that yet other derivations have been reported. Readers interested in delving into this technical issue are referred to Algom, D. (2021). The Weber–Fechner law: A misnomer that persists but that should go away. *Psychological Review,* 128, 757–768; and Masin, S. C., Zudini, V., and Antonelli, M. (2009). Early alternative derivations of Fechner's Law. *Journal of the History of the Behavioral Sciences,* 45, 56–65.

7. The formula is the "formal expression" of Fechner's Law. In handbooks of perception, the law is often also shown in the simplified form ("habitual expression") $s = c \cdot \log(I)$. This simplified version is obtained by assuming that the absolute threshold is equal to the unit, thus $\log(I/1) = \log(I)$. This assumption is totally legitimate given that, with a suitable operation, it is always possible to change the scale of measurement of I so that $I_0 = 1$. In mathematical terms it makes no difference, but in terms of understanding the meaning of the law it makes a huge difference, and at least in my experience this is a point that many people will miss if it is left implicit.

8. Another technical point should be made here. There is a subtle difference between stating that differential thresholds and reference intensities stand in a constant ratio (Weber's Law), and stating that equal increments in sensation correspond to equal ratios between physical stimuli (Fechner's). The former is a statement about two physical quantities, whereas the latter corresponds to stating that psychological sensations are a function of stimulus ratios, that is, that psychological quantities are relational in nature. It has been argued that the second statement should be called Weber's *prin-*

ciple, and that Fechner's derivation was actually based on Weber's principle rather than on Weber's Law.
9. To be more precise, duration should also be specified, given that other conditions being equal, longer sounds tend to be perceived as more intense. In addition, the distance from the sound source should be specified as the energy of a sound wave is reduced in proportion to the square of the distance between source and receiver. For instance, each time the distance doubles, the perceived intensity drops by around 6 decibels.
10. The classic reference on this is Jastrow, J. (1887). The psycho-physic law and star magnitudes. *The American Journal of Psychology*, 1, 112–127.
11. In the psychophysical literature, the notion of jnd is often used to refer both to the psychological unit (how many jnd is this sensation above the reference value?) and to the difference threshold (how much should the physical stimulus be increased to make the difference noticeable?). This is confusing, as the qualifier "just-noticeable" implies *noticing*, a psychological process. For this reason, a distinction is sometimes made between *sensation jnd* (the first meaning) and *stimulus jnd* (the second).
12. Hartline, H.K. and Graham, C.H.(1932). *Nerve Impulses from Single Receptors in the Eye, Journal of Cellular and Comparative Physiology*, 1, 277–295.
13. Selig Hecht was born in 1892 in a town that was then in the Prussian empire (today in Poland), but emigrated to the USA with his family when he was six. He worked almost all his life at Columbia University in New York City. The work I refer to here is Hecht, S. (1924) The Visual Discrimination of Intensity and the Weber-Fechner Law, *Journal of General Physiology*, 7, 235–267.
14. Stanley Smith Stevens (1906–1972) made many fundamental contributions to the theory of measurement, not only in psychophysics but also generally in applied statistics. The *Handbook of Experimental Psychology*, first edited by Stevens in 1951, quickly became one of the main references for the subject. The fourth edition, now entitled *Steven's Handbook of Experimental Psychology and Cognitive Neuroscience*, was published in five volumes in 2018.
15. Stevens, S.S. (1957). On the Psychophysical Law, *Psychological Review*, 64, 153–181.
16. *Ibidem*, p. 153.
17. In a nutshell, the idea is that that some experimental outcomes are best attributed to sensory processes, others are best attributed to judgement processes, and yet other results can be viewed equally well from either perspective. The alternatives each have special advantages, and can be taken as complementary and mutually completing. A good example of this idea is found in Baird, J. C. (1997). *Sensation and judgement: Complementarity theory of psychophysics*. Lawrence Erlbaum Associates, Inc.

CHAPTER 3

The Doors of Perception

Abstract The key idea of psychophysics is that mental contents can be assessed by studying discrimination in classical psychophysics; this is done by measuring thresholds. However, the notion of threshold, and especially of absolute threshold, is in many ways problematic. These problems led to psychophysical approaches that dispense with the notion of threshold, although they preserve the spirit of Weber's original idea. These modern developments yielded further developments which ultimately turned useful to assess desire.

Keywords Pirenne's experiment • Psychometric function • Inner psychophysics • Adaptation level

The Doors were a cult band of the classic rock era.[1] Many fans know that the group's name comes from the title of an essay written by the British author Aldous Huxley,[2] *The Doors of Perception*. In the essay, Huxley was concerned with the philosophical implications of his own experiences under the influence of mescaline, a subject that was destined to become dear to the Sixties countercultures. Overcoming mental limits to reach true essences was indeed a common topic in many works of the group's poet-singer Jim Morrison. For instance, a line of his poem *Power* reads, "I can perceive events on other worlds, in my deepest inner mind and in the minds of others". The final verses of *Break On Through (To The Other*

Side), one of the band's greatest hits, mentions a straight, deep, and wide gate—inviting us to break on through to the other side. However, the expression in the book title was not actually invented by Huxley; it comes from a passage in William Blake's book mentioned in the previous chapter.

In *Marriage of Heaven and Hell*, after reflecting on the senses, Blake noted how this leads us to understand that the body and soul are not separate, and concluded: "If the doors of perception were cleansed everything would appear to man as it is, infinite". He was implying that a special location lies somewhere between mind and matter, a door of perception that we can enter—and go from the world of the imperceptible to the world of consciousness. This idea is as fascinating to us as it was, presumably, to Blake, Huxley, and Morrison. But do these doors really exist? And if so, what are they? As an influential researcher from the University of California in San Diego, John Wixted stated, many people have a "naïve theory of threshold", meaning that they indeed believe that there are critical values in the intensity of a stimulus, such that below these values there is no conscious sensation.

For instance, many of us give credit to myths about influencing purchasing behaviour by "subliminal" messages included in a film or TV programme.[3] As we saw in the previous chapter, the concept of threshold plays a fundamental role in Fechner's Law, both with reference to absolute threshold—understood as the physical intensity beneath which the sensation is zero—and in the concept of differential threshold as a unit of measurement for sensations. In some dimensions of physical stimulation, these concepts are useful for building sensation models. The development of modern psychophysics has however forced us to admit that things don't always work in this way. This is because the models don't always work so well in other dimensions, but also because more sophisticated analyses have confronted us with a series of thorny problems in the very concept of sensory threshold.

Sensing Degree Zero

One interesting way of examining the problems inherent in the concept of threshold is to wonder how we could measure a threshold that is truly absolute, an authentic "door of perception" corresponding to the minimum physical intensity that an organism can perceive. In an experiment conducted in the early 1940s,[4] the Belgian physicist Maurice Henri Pirenne sought to respond precisely to this question in the field of vision.

To understand his results, we need to spend a few words on his apparatus used and measuring methods. In building his experimental apparatus, Pirenne took stock on what was already known, at the time of the study, on how the eye captures the light and transforms it into a neural signal sent to the brain. In this way, the participants' eyes in the experiment had the maximum probability of being able to capture a very small light intensity. The method he used to measure the threshold, on the other hand, was simply one of the methods described by Fechner in *Elemente*. It is worth examining both these aspects in detail.

As concerns the first aspect, let us start from well-established facts. As we know, we can see well during the day, when there is plenty of light. But we can also see at night, usually thanks to the fact that some light comes from the moon or the stars (assuming there is no artificial light). Yet we don't see during the day and at night in exactly the same way. During the day, we can see colours and make out details; at night, we are only able to see rough shapes that all appear in a more or less bright shade of grey. Furthermore, if we pass quickly from day to night, the experience is very different from when we pass from night to day. Imagine walking along a mountain footpath in the midday sun. You reach an unlit tunnel in the rock, enter and keep on walking. You will have the feeling of not being able to see anything at all, and you will probably have to stop for a few seconds, as this feeling lasts quite a long time. Only after a while will you be able to distinguish shapes and walk with more confidence. If you are a good observer, at this point you will also perhaps begin to notice that shapes can be distinguished better if you look at them out of the corner of your eye. The neural basis for this phenomenon is well understood and depends on the anatomy and functional characteristics of the retina, the thin layer at the rear of the eye where we find the photoreceptors, the nerve cells that turn light into a neural signal.

There are two types of retinal photoreceptors: cones and rods. Cones enable us to see colours, but rods do not, for reasons that we will ignore in this book.[5] What matters here is the response of cones and rods to light intensity and their distribution on the surface of the retina. Cones are fairly insensitive to very low intensities, while rods respond precisely to these intensities, and at greater intensities they are disabled (in technical terms, they "saturate"). Cones are therefore optimised for daytime vision, and rods for nighttime vision. Furthermore, both types of photoreceptors change their sensitivity according to light intensity. This gradual change is called adaptation. The reason why, when we enter a dark tunnel, it takes time to be able to see something is because rod adaptation is a slow process, which takes considerable time (up to 20 minutes for full adaptation). Finally, cones and rods are distributed differently on the retina. Cones are concentrated mostly in a central area, the fovea, where they are very small and densely packed into a very tight mosaic. There are no rods in the fovea. Rods are instead denser around the sides of the fovea. When we look at an object during the day, we move our eyes to project the object on the fovea. This is why, due to the density of the cones in that point, during the day we can see fine details. But if we want to look at an object in the dark, we have to look sideways, because in this way we use the area where the rods are densest.

As you will have understood, if we try to find the absolute threshold of vision, we have to create the optimal conditions for the rods to function. To create these conditions in Pirenne's experiment, before starting each session the participants had to spend 30 minutes in the dark, to adapt the rods in the best possible way. In each experiment, a luminous disc was presented for a very short time, lit by a beam at the wavelength of maximum rod sensitivity (more or less in the centre of the visible spectrum). In addition, participants were required to stare not directly at the disc but at a point slightly to one side of it. This guaranteed that the light of the disc stimulated the area of the retina with the highest rod concentration, thus maximising the probability of a neural response. Finally, the presented light intensities were extremely low, in fact so low that Pirenne did not measure them in the commonly used photometric units but as the number of light quanta[6] coming from the disc.

With this apparatus, Pirenne estimated the absolute threshold using one of the methods described by Fechner in *Elemente*, the so-called method of constant stimuli. He selected six levels of intensity for the disc (from 20 to 400 light quanta) and presented them many times in random order. This is precisely the reason for the name of this method: the stimuli are constant as they are pre-set and are always the same, even though they are presented in different sequences each time. In every experimental session, the observers simply had to say if they saw something, replying "yes" or "no". At the end, Pirenne counted the number of positive replies for each of the six levels of intensity and divided it by the corresponding total number of presentations. In this way, he obtained six measurements of the proportion of "yes" responses as a function of intensity. By studying these measurements, he found that the participants said yes practically every time more than 200 quanta were presented, and practically always no when less than 100 quanta were presented. Between 100 and 200 quanta, there was an area of uncertainty where the probability of replying yes or no was more or less equivalent, with minor shifts towards one of the two alternatives.

Reflecting on this result, Pirenne and his research group reached a surprising conclusion. Remember that the area of uncertainty measured in the study refers to the light presented on the disc. Before reaching the rods on the retina, this light must cross a certain space and pass through the structures in the eye. For instance, it must cross the lens. Considering the fact that some light quanta in the path are lost due to dispersion, reflection, or absorption, Pirenne and his collaborators calculated that of the 100–200 quanta coming from the disc, not more than 5–14 actually reached the rods. And this is where it gets interesting. Given that so few quanta reached the rods, Pirenne thought, and given that there are very many rods, it is very unlikely for two quanta to end up on the same rod. Therefore, in the experimental conditions, only one quantum of light needed to reach only one rod to obtain a positive response, provided that this occurred at the same time in 5–14 other rods. At least for vision, sensing degree zero is therefore so low that it touches the limits set by the corpuscular structure of light.

And things are not very different when considering other perceptual modalities. The great Hungarian physiologist Georg von Békésy[7] calculated that the absolute threshold for a sound corresponds to a vibration one hundred times smaller than the diameter of the orbit of an electron around the nucleus of a hydrogen atom. The entity of this vibration is therefore so small that, once again, it lies at the very limit of the structure of matter. If we consider another way of responding to mechanical stimulation, touch, it is often reported that the absolute threshold corresponds to the pressure exerted by the wing of a fly dropped from a height of one centimetre onto a person's cheek. For smell and taste, making estimations is more complicated. If you do some research, you will probably read that the threshold for an odour is equivalent to a drop of perfume in a 150 square-metre apartment, or that the threshold for taste is a teaspoon of sugar dissolved in four litres of water. But clearly these examples have a rather limited meaning, as sensitivity depends on the chemical compound considered.

If you think about it, however, this fact is valid not only for chemical senses, but generally concerns the issue of absolute threshold. For example, the threshold for touch is different if, rather than considering the skin on the cheek, we take measurements on the palm or belly. In addition, it changes with age, and according to some studies also depends on sex—it goes without saying that women are deemed to have greater tactile sensitivity. In the case of hearing, von Békésy's estimation is valid only for a vibration at 3000 Hz. As we saw in the previous chapter, auditory sensitivity depends not only on the amplitude of a vibration but also on its frequency. And, of course, as we saw in detail above, the absolute threshold of vision can only be measured in very specific situations. Having to develop a very complicated experimental apparatus, Pirenne knew something about this.

All this suggests that the concept of threshold poses a number of problems. In certain very specific conditions, the absolute threshold can be found at such weak intensities that it makes no sense to think of it as a door of perception. In these cases, going through that door we would find nothing on the other side, because we are practically at the limits set by physics. In everyday life, whether or not we perceive a sensation will depend on many other things besides the stimulus intensity itself. Ok, you will say, let's forget about the idea of absolute threshold. But is it not still true that, having specified the conditions, there will be some levels of intensity that will not produce conscious sensations and others that will? Perhaps, rather than an ultimate "door" of perception, as William Blake intended it, there are many doors, depending on the situation. Was this not Fechner's reasoning, after all, when he used jnds as a unit of measurement for sensation? Here too, however, things are more complicated.

An Elusive Door

To understand what we precisely mean when we talk of thresholds in psychophysics, imagine visiting Henri Pirenne's laboratory. Pirenne has just finished an experimental session and is looking at a graph displaying the results.[8] Let's look at it with him: Fig. 3.1 shows six dots, which correspond to the proportion of times the participant reported seeing the flash of light (on the y-axis) according to the six levels of intensity presented during the sessions (on the x-axis). Using appropriate statistical methods, we can identify the mathematical law describing the relationship between the two variables. You may think of this law as a curve that summarises how the variable on the y-axis changes according to the variation on the x-axis. In the figure, this is the S shaped curve, "sigmoid" because the plot shows this s-shaped progression. When the light intensity is low (the first

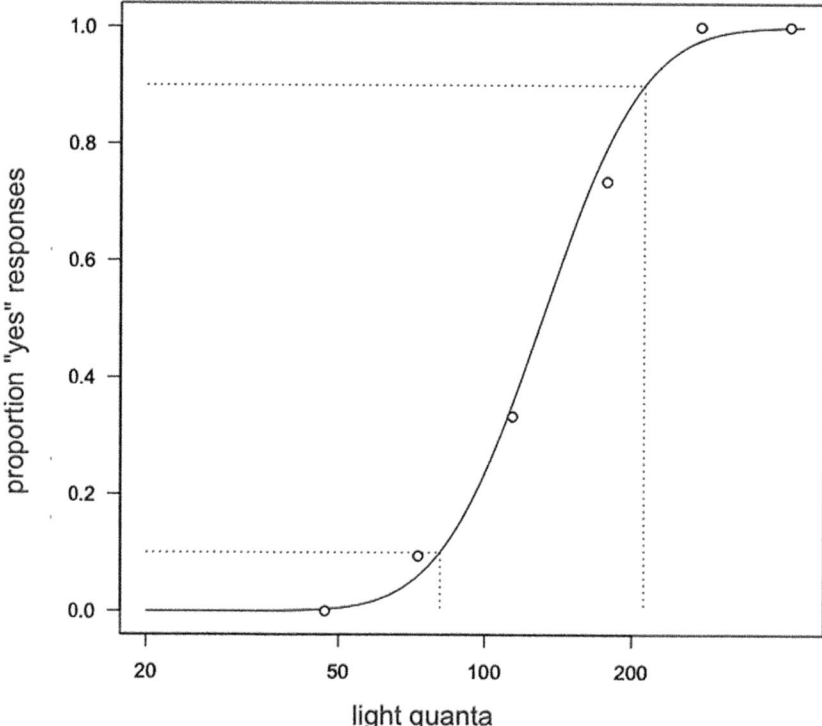

Fig. 3.1 The results of one of Pirenne's experimental sessions. In each trial, the participant saw one of six possible discs illuminated with 47, 73, 114, 178, 276, or 421 light quanta. The dots show the proportion of "yes" answers (the participant states that they saw the disc) according to these six levels of intensity. The S-shaped curve is fitted to the six dots to estimate the proportions for all the other possible intensity values on the x-axis. This curve, known in psychophysics as the *psychometric function*, represents the correct way of defining the concept of threshold in psychophysics: as a mathematical model of uncertainty

two dots) the participant almost always says "no". When it is high (the last two dots), they almost always say "yes". In the middle, there is uncertainty: in the case of the third dot, the observer said yes around 40% of the times; for the fourth, around 75% of the times. However, these data offer limited information, not only because there are just six dots but also because the data are "dirty".

By this I don't wish to say that there is necessarily something wrong in the data, merely that there is a limit to the precision with which we can measure the proportion of positive answers. Every measurement, even the most precise, is always affected by a certain percentage of error simply due to chance, and the effect of chance becomes clear if we repeat the experimental sessions: presumably, the data will be similar to the previous one, but not exactly the same. The *S*-shaped function comes into play precisely for these reasons. Using the mathematical model, we obtain a representation of the relationship between the two variables that kills two birds with one curve. On one hand, we get rid of the detritus of random errors, cleansing our measurements and obtaining an elegant view of the overall trend. On the other, we can estimate the probability of response not only for the effectively measured intensities but also for any value in the domain of the function.

For instance, we could reason in these terms: let's assume that, in operational terms, "being sure of not having seen the light" means that the participant says yes less than one time out of ten, and that "being sure of having seen it" means answering yes more than nine times out of ten. On the basis of this definition, we can define an area of uncertainty, which is that shown by the two vertical lines (roughly between 70 and 200 quanta). Pirenne's conclusions on absolute threshold are based on this area of uncertainty. But what exactly is the threshold? In the famous article we began with, Pirenne estimated it to be around 150 quanta. If you observe the figure, 150 light quanta is the intensity at which the proportion of positive answers is 0.6, or 60%. At this value, it is just slightly more probable that there is a positive answer than a negative answer, but it is clear that the negative answers are far from infrequent.

In fact, Pirenne could have chosen other values to estimate the threshold, and such choice would have been equally legitimate. He could have chosen that in which the proportion increases to 0.9, more or less where we leave the area of uncertainty and the disc is seen practically every time. Or that in which the proportion is exactly 0.5, which corresponds to the point of maximum uncertainty—half the times, the observer states that they saw the disc, but the other half says the opposite. The point is that there is no fixed intensity at which we cross through the "door of perception", passing from the absence of consciousness to consciousness. In psychophysics, when we estimate the threshold with a single number, we do so being fully aware of the fact that it is merely a conventional point of reference, which can be useful for making comparisons with other situations. The observer's answer obeys a probabilistic law, and only the curve as a whole represents this completely.

The elusive nature of the psychophysical threshold leads us to pose some interesting questions. One of these concerns the variability of answers in the area of uncertainty. When the stimulus is in that area, what causes the participant to think that they have seen something in some cases and that they have not in others? As mentioned above, each measurement is affected by a random error, but this error of measurement is cancelled out with statistics. Thus, the curve estimates the sigmoidal trend of the answer, purified of this type of error. And yet the answer still obeys a probabilistic principle. Another question concerns the existence of an actual absolute threshold. Does a degree zero of sensation, an intensity below which the observer never perceives anything, exist? Modern psychophysics has offered profoundly counterintuitive answers to this question, which takes us again on a different level, that of the neural processes responsible for coding the input physical stimulus.

The Sound of Silence

Consider the following scenario. While you are busy doing something, you feel your mobile phone vibrating in your pocket. It must be a text message or some other notification. You take your phone out but, surprisingly, you have no messages at all. This has happened to me several times. According to the literature, it's quite a common phenomenon, and indeed it has even earned its own technical name, "phantom vibration syndrome".[9] Again according to the literature, there is also an acoustic version, the illusory sensation of hearing the phone ring. This form of the phenomenon appears to have been less studied, but this has also happened to me once or twice.

So what happens in these situations? Hallucination? Suggestion? The unconscious desire to be contacted by someone special? Perhaps, but one of the fundamental rules of science is the economy principle, according to which the simplest explanation for a phenomenon should always be preferred to more complicated alternatives. In our case, a simple explanation comes from physiology. Nerve cells dialogue with each other, exchanging electric signals. In some cases, these signals can be modulated by an input stimulus, in others by signals from other cells. The signal modulation may be in the direction of excitation or inhibition, depending on a whole series of factors that here we can ignore. The point is that it is a matter of modulation, i.e., a change in the activity of a cell in relation to its level of spontaneous activity. This activity is always there, an omnipresent background noise subject to statistical fluctuations. It is this background noise which comes to the fore in certain cases, and we mistake it for a weak signal we think we have perceived.

These facts have clear implications for the concept of sensory threshold. If the response of an organism depends on an internal signal that is affected by random variations, it is reasonable to expect that, in a "window of uncertainty", a given stimulus intensity may lead to positive responses in some cases but to negative ones in others. Therefore, we will never be able to identify a specific point between the absence of sensation and the awareness of something. The transition can happen within a range of stimulus intensities, and all we can try to estimate are the corresponding probabilities. In addition, and this is the most counterintuitive aspect, it is in principle possible to have sensations without stimuli, as is the case with phantom vibration. The phenomenon is therefore not a hallucination, but simply the consequence of random variations in spontaneous activity. Precisely because these variations are governed by chance, they are mostly minute, but can occasionally be more noticeable. When this happens, it is possible that they can even activate a response, and therefore, as Paul Simon and Art Garfunkel sang, we hear the sound of silence.

The idea that there can be sensation even without stimulus is key to modern psychophysics. The underlying idea is however much older. In fact, while observing neural noise became possible only in the second half of last century, when methods were developed for recording from nerve fibres, the first mathematical model of how chance can determine the outcome of a comparison between sensations dates back to none other than one of the main protagonists of this book, Gustav Theodor Fechner. Today, textbooks remember Fechner for the psychophysical function that bears his name. However, in addition to the problem of the functional relationship between physical stimulus and psychological response, in *Elemente* Fechner also tackled the problem of the relationship between stimulus and the response of the nervous system. Fechner defined the former as the domain of "outer" psychophysics, and the latter as that of "inner" psychophysics.[10] Fechner's work on inner psychophysics was in many respects even more pioneering than that on the psychophysical function. Fechner in fact managed to build a mathematical model that not only envisages the possibility of phantom sensations, but also offers a general description of how a sensory system can perceive the difference between two stimuli. This second idea was destined to be rediscovered in the following century, eventually becoming one of the cornerstones of the methods used to quantify desire.

Fechner's core idea was that each activation of the sensory system depends on the sum of two factors: the effect of the input stimulus and a certain percentage of random measurement error. But which laws govern this measurement error? Thanks to the German mathematician Johann Carl Friedrich Gauss, Fechner knew that random measurement error can be modelled by a bell-shaped probability distribution—the Gaussian curve. According to Gauss, each measurement observed using any instrument can be thought of as the sum of two components

$$O_i = M \pm E_i$$

where O is the value observed in the measurement identified by i (in the first measurement $i = 1$, in the second $i = 2$, and so on), E is the random error associated with that specific i-nth measurement, and M is a constant that corresponds to the measurement without error, i.e., when $O = M$, or, if you prefer, when the observation corresponds to the "true value" of the thing we are measuring. However, if you think about it, it is not clear what this might mean, given that we can only know the value of our measurements and not the "real" thing we wish to measure. Whenever we take a measurement, the value of E is unknown, so it could be any number. Gauss, however, understood that there is something we can know about these errors, and this is the probability that they are more or less big. Gauss demonstrated that the most probable errors are the small ones, those which shift the measurement from the "true" value only slightly. He demonstrated that the magnitude of errors is distributed as a bell-shaped curve. The central part of the bell has errors close to zero, they are small errors, and these errors are the most probable. Moving away from the centre, the probability decreases more and more, following a bell shape. As the curve is symmetrical in relation to its centre, the negative and positive errors cancel each other out, and their sums tend to zero. For this reason, if I repeat the measurement many times, even if I will never be able to know which errors I have made with each measurement, I can be sure that, by calculating the average of all the measurements taken, these errors will tend to cancel each other out, and increasingly so the more measurements I take.

The mathematical formula describing the Gaussian curve is rather complicated, at least for non-specialists, but what we are interested in here is that this formula contains a parameter that measures dispersion, i.e., the typical amplitude of the errors observable in practice.[11] This parameter is σ, the *standard deviation* of the distribution. Imagine having to weigh an object, and having two analogue scales. These scales are charming vintage pieces and are not easy to use because the weight is read from a graduated scale on a lever arm, on the end of which there is a plate on which you place the object to weigh. Suppose you take around 20 measurements with the first scale, and that you find that the measurements fall between 9.9 and 10.1. Then you take the same measurements with the second scale; and here you find that the measurements fall between 9.5 and 10.5. The range of errors observed seems to be smaller with the first than with the second scale. But there is a problem: you don't know where the scales come from, and therefore you don't know the unit of measurement engraved on the lever arm. Perhaps the first is European-made, and in this case the range of error would be 0.2 kilogrammes, while the second is USA-made, where in many cases the metric decimal system is not used. In this second case, the range could be 1 ounce, which is equal to around 0.03 kilogrammes, so in fact the range of error is far smaller.

This is important because the observed range of error gives us some precious information: the smaller the range, the higher the precision of the scales. The problem therefore lies in being able to find a way to measure precision that can be comparable in the two cases, i.e., a common unit of measurement. This can be done using the parameter σ. Let's assume that the standard deviation is 0.1 kilogramme in the first case and 0.5 kilogramme in the second. Expressed in the same unit of measurement using the standard deviation, the ranges of error will be $0.2/0.1 = 2\,\sigma$ in the first case and again $1/0.5 = 2\,\sigma$ in the second. Therefore, even if we don't know the units of measurement used to measure the weight, in this case we would conclude that the two scales are equally precise. If the σ parameters were different, of course we could have concluded otherwise. The point is that the standard deviation provides an "intrinsic" unit of measurement for the distribution of the observed values, without having to know the original one.

Fechner extended Gauss's theory of error to the problem of measuring sensations. Just as scales are instruments for measuring weight, in the same way a given sensory system can be considered an instrument that measures some form of stimulating energy. And just like any other measurement, neural noise adds a certain amount of error to each measurement. The actual error associated with each measurement remains unknown, but Gauss's model allows us to reconstruct its probability distribution in a sample of independent measurements. Using this model, we can explain phantom vibration and offer a theory of how the perceptual system assesses the difference between two stimuli.

Looking at Fig. 3.2, which shows the two hypothetical distributions of neural activation in the two cases considered, i.e., when no vibration is administered (top) and when vibration of intensity A is administered (bottom). In the first case, the effect of the vibration should be zero (given that there is none). Yet the activation is never zero, due to random neural noise. The bell curve describes the probability distribution of that noise, which will sometimes be lower and sometimes higher than the peak of distribution, the most probable noise level. When the vibration is present, on the other hand, the distribution is exactly the same, but the noise is above or below A, the effect of the vibration. The distribution is simply shifted to the right by an amount equal to A. Fechner proposed that there is conscious sensation when the level of internal activation exceeds a critical value, given by the average of the two distributions. This is the intermediate value between A and 0, indicated in the figure by $d/2$. When there is no vibration, but the noise happens to exceed $d/2$, we therefore feel a phantom vibration.

However, Fechner's model did not only predict that in some cases we should hear the sound of silence. The model described in Fig. 3.2 is valid for any pair of stimuli, not only in the special case in which one of the two is zero. Look at the figure again, and imagine that the top curve describes the distribution of the activation when a vibration of B, less than A, is administered. We can reason in exactly the same way we did for the phantom vibration: in this case, we investigate the probability that vibration B, physically less than A, is instead perceived as greater. In the model, this probability is equal to the grey area to the right of $d/2$, in the top curve in the figure. Fechner's brilliant intuition was to note that the distance d, in the theoretical model, can be interpreted as the measurement of the increase in sensation produced by A, compared to the sensation produced by B.

Here, once again, we find ourselves facing the fundamental problem of psychophysics. These sensations are by definition private and accessible only to the person who feels them. However, Fechner observed that the increase from A to B can be measured in the intrinsic unit of the two

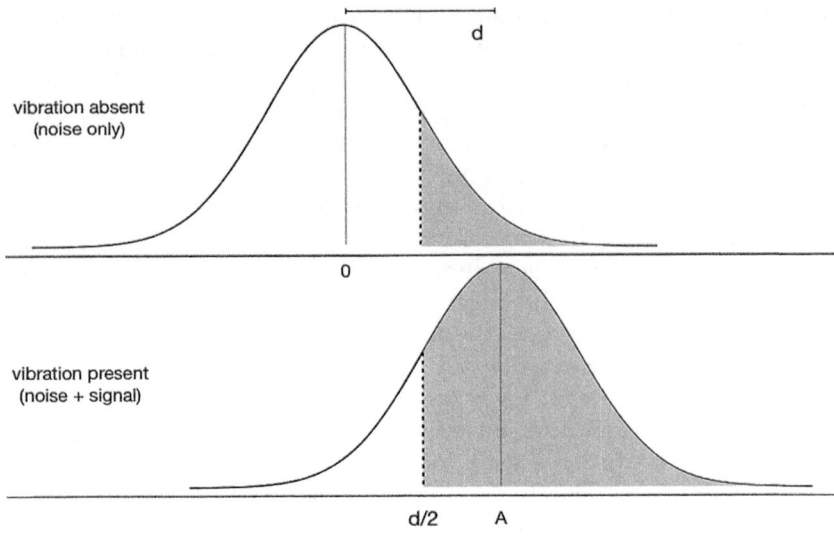

Fig. 3.2 Phantom vibration in Fechner's inner psychophysics. Imagine two different situations: in the first (top line) there is no vibration; in the second (bottom line), there is a vibration with intensity A. The curves represent the variability of internal activation, given by the value of the physical vibration (top, 0; below, A, shown by the dotted segments) plus the random variability of the neural signals. The area below the "Gaussian" bell-shaped curve represents the relative probability of the magnitude of the error. Fechner proposed that there is conscious sensation when internal activations exceed the intermediate value between the peaks of the two distributions ($d/2$, i.e., the average of the activations in the two cases, the dotted segments). In this way, the grey area to the right of $d/2$ in the two curves represents the probability of an activation above that reference level. If the vibration is actually present (bottom curve), the model predicts that this activation will produce a real sensation. If it is absent (top curve), the model predicts that it will produce a phantom vibration

distributions, i.e., in dispersion units σ. Without going into detail, this is the point: the Gaussian curve is described analytically by a mathematical formula (density function), which gives us the height of the curve, on the y-axis, for each value on the x-axis of the graph. For instance, in the middle of the curve we see that it reaches its maximum height, whereas moving towards the left and right the height gradually drops to zero. Now let's consider an interval defined by two values on the *x*-axis. For instance, look at the figure again, and the interval between A and infinite on the bottom curve (grey area). This interval defines an area, which we can think of as the sum of all the infinitesimal heights for all the (infinite) points on the curve corresponding to the (infinite) values between A and infinite on the *x*-axis. This area is the curve integral, and the interesting thing is that we can also do the opposite: just as we can calculate the area starting from the underlying interval on the *x*-axis, by inverting the calculation, from the area we can find the interval and therefore the value of A, expressed in units of dispersion σ.

The difference between the two sensations evoked by B and A, in units that are "private and accessible only to the person feeling them", thus becomes measurable in units of dispersion σ. Now we just have to note that the unknown area we have represented in the figure can be estimated with an experiment. All we have to do is present the two stimuli many times, asking an observer which is the most intense vibration. In accordance with the model, due to neuronal noise, when I present B in a certain percentage of the tests the observer will report the illusory sensation that B is greater than A. This percentage represents an estimate of the size of the grey area (in the top curve), compared to the total area of the curve. When I present A, in the same way I can calculate the same percentage of times in which the observer reports the—in this case, correct—sensation that A is greater than B. In this way, I can find A and B from the two areas in units of dispersion σ, and therefore their difference. Job done.

A Gateless Gate

The measurement of sensation developed by Fechner in the field of "internal" psychophysics seems very different from those using Fechner's Law for external psychophysics. In this case, sensation is measured on an absolute scale, starting at a point that corresponds to an actual zero, i.e., the absence of sensation. On the contrary, in the model described in the previous paragraph we do not have to assume that this point exists. Thus, psychophysics without a concept of absolute threshold becomes possible. It is worth reflecting on the implications of this change of perspective. If, on one hand, we can now avoid all the difficulties implicit in measuring thresholds, on the other we have to give up on the idea that the intensity of the sensation is an absolute quantity that can be interpreted as a valid measurement in any situation. Instead, we have to replace it with the idea that what determines the contents of mental life is a fundamentally relational process. The effect of a stimulus can be measured only as a change compared to a reference value that is constantly variable depending on the conditions.

This method is still based on Weber's fundamental intuition: by studying discrimination capacity, we can relate variations in stimuli with variations in the corresponding psychological effects. The change of perspective is nonetheless significant. That which in classical psychophysics, and in the naive psychology of many of us, was an authentic "door of perception", now looks far more like the elusive "gateless" gate[12] that according to some eastern philosophies we must pass through on the road to enlightenment.

Fechner's intuition was destined to trigger many twentieth century developments in psychophysics. These approaches also differ precisely in how they interpret the meaning of the reference value in relation to which the relative intensity of sensation is measured.[13] The most relevant to the story I am telling here came from the US psychologist Harry Helson, who presented it for the first time in a famous work published soon after the end of the Second World War.[14] In contrast to the approach of classical psychophysics, in which the measurement of sensation was thought of as the study of the relationship between a single stimulus and the corresponding sensory response, in Helson's approach the response does not depend on a single stimulus but rather on the comparison with the overall configuration of the stimulation. According to Helson, the latter has three components: the specific stimulus relevant for the sensation being measured (for instance, the intensity of a sound), all the other stimuli present at the same time (other sounds), and the "history" of the stimulation (sounds presented previously). The set of these three components sets an *adaptation level* in the system, corresponding to the overall effect on the organism of the set of stimulations it is exposed to.

According to Helson, there is a specific level of adaptation for each stimulation condition, and the adaptation changes continuously according to the spatial and temporal context, defining a reference level in relation to which the effect of each new stimulus is assessed. Furthermore, Helson deemed the concept to be valid in general, such that it could be used to measure sensations associated with any kind of object taken into consideration. Starting from the 1950s, adaption-level theory was thus applied in many fields of psychological studies, including learning, personality, intelligence, motivation, and affective valence. Concerning the latter, in particular, new theories began to suggest that decisions could be studied in relation to the positive or negative valence triggered by upward or downward deviations from an adaption level.[15] Helson's theory reached the height of its popularity in the early Sixties, when the prestigious American Psychological Association (the APA also established one of the most commonly used formats for articles published in scientific literature) honoured him with the Distinguished Scientific Contribution Award for "having conducted significant research to solve a wide range of problems, from colour vision to social processes".

Yet the influence of Helson's theory was not confined within the boundaries of psychology. From the Sixties, the theory was also used by economists and social scientists. One intriguing application concerns the problem of measuring happiness, i.e., the degree of subjective satisfaction an individual gains from possessing an object or achieving a certain state of things. In this context, the concept of hedonic relativism[16] came to the fore, the idea that the happiness of an individual, or that of society as a whole, is not an absolute value but is fundamentally relational, and for this reason also intrinsically elusive. For the hedonic relativist, the experience of happiness is always determined by a comparison with a reference state, that is, an adaptation level. Thus, we all live on a sort of hedonic treadmill, forced to chase increasingly higher levels of stimulation in order to maintain a constant level of happiness. However, the understanding of these mechanisms can teach us how to seek happiness wisely, both at individual and collective levels. In social policies, this means understanding that what determines the level of happiness is first and foremost our comparison with a context acting as the *status quo*, and that this is defined powerfully by the mass media. But this issue goes way beyond the purposes of this book. To finally reach the law of desire, we must now learn how some of the ideas of classic psychophysics were in some sense anticipated in the field of economics.

Notes

1. The Doors were active for around a decade between the 1960s and '70s. They are considered to be one of the most influential bands of *art rock*, a sub-genre of rock that sought to go beyond the typical pop song framework, incorporating more complex and ambitious musical forms derived from classical music, jazz, and folk.

2. Aldous Huxley is best known for his great dystopic science-fiction novel *Brave New World*, published in 1932. He was the grandson of one of the most influential British biologists of the nineteenth century, Thomas Huxley, a renowned advocate of Darwin's theory of evolution.
3. In the late Fifties, the media reported the results of an experiment on the effect of subliminal messages. Reportedly, single low-contrast images with the messages "drink Coca-Cola" and "eat popcorn" were inserted in a film shown in a cinema. These messages supposedly increased the sales of Coca-Cola and popcorn among the cinema-goers. Later, the author admitted that he had invented the whole thing. Despite this, the matter continues to fuel conspiracy theories, and many countries still have laws forbidding the use of subliminal techniques in advertising.
4. Hecht, S., Shlaer , S. and Pirenne, M.H. (1942) *Energy, Quanta, and Vision. Journal of General Physiology*, 25, pp. 819–840.
5. On this matter, see, for instance, Palmer, S. E. (1999). *Vision science: Photons to phenomenology.* The MIT Press.
6. One counterintuitive aspect of how physics describes that which we commonly call light is that some phenomena are better captured by an undulatory description, as if light were a wave that oscillates within a certain frequency, while others are better captured by a corpuscular description, in which electromagnetic energy consists of discrete packages known as light *quanta* or *photons*. The behaviour of photoreceptors in the retina can be interpreted as that of a mechanism that effectively "counts" the number of photons detected.
7. The great Hungarian neurophysiologist Georg von Békésy (1879–1972) received the Nobel Prize for Medicine in 1961, "for his discoveries of the physical mechanism of stimulation within the cochlea". The cochlea is the part of the inner ear that houses the hearing receptors.
8. All the data of Pirenne's experiment are public and can be downloaded from the web. Those of the session in Fig. 3.1 refer to observer S.H., Selig Hecht, the physiologist mentioned at the end of the previous chapter. Hecht authored the publication of the famous experiment with Pirenne and his assistant at Columbia University, Simon Shlaer.
9. Rosenberger, R. (2015) An Experiential Account of Phantom Vibration Syndrome, *Computers in Human Behaviour,* 52, 124–131.
10. Fechner's notion of inner psychophysics was largely ignored in the heyday of the field. However, Fechner believed that inner psychophysics in fact provided the theoretical reason for why Weber's and his laws applied to psychology, that is, that it provided the needed bridge between neural and mental events. In the second volume of *Elemente,* Fechner developed this idea at length. See Murray, D.J. and Link, S.W. (2021) *The creation of scientific psychology,* Routledge, pp. 98–104.

11. The function of a Gaussian probability distribution is defined for all real values between minus infinite and plus infinite. For a mathematician, there is a non-null probability for any error, be it small or large. For errors larger or smaller than 4 standard deviations, however, the probability becomes so small that, in practice, it is null.
12. For example, one of the fundamental texts of Zen Buddhism is the *Mumonkan* (*The Gateless Gate*), attributed to Master Wumen who lived between the twelfth and thirteenth centuries. The text is a collection of 48 "koans", enigmatic and paradoxical short stories on which students meditate on their own personal path to enlightenment. Access to this state of superior consciousness requires rejecting, and therefore transcending, the dualism between mind and matter that we implicitly adopt when using language to categorise the contents of consciousness. Access is for this reason through a "gateless" gate. Some of the koans in *Mumonkan* became popular within scientific circles, thanks to Douglas Hofstadter's brilliant essay *Gödel, Escher, Bach: An Eternal Golden Braid* (Penguin books, 1979), where some aspects of Zen are used to discuss the paradoxes that emerge in the cognitive sciences when thinking about concepts such as form, meaning, and truth.
13. Perhaps the most important consists of interpreting the reference value as a response criterion adopted by the observer. This approach, known as "signal detection theory", originated from work in electronics (in particular, concerning the interpretation of radar signals). The fundamental idea is that when we have to decide on the presence of a signal (e.g., "can we see a plane in the radar?"), the operator's answer depends on two factors. One is automatic, unconscious, and sensory-based, whereas the other depends on a conscious decision. To decide which answer to give ("yes, I can see a plane", or "no, I can't see a plane"), operators establish a criterion, the degree of subjective confidence above which they are willing to give a positive answer. Using appropriate statistical models, it is possible to measure this criterion and, independently thereof, the level of sensory sensitivity. This approach continues to be of great importance in studying the effectiveness of diagnostic systems in medicine (such as the interpretation of x-rays or magnetic resonance images).
14. Helson, H. (1947) Adaptation Level as a Frame of Reference for the Prediction of Psychophysical Data, *American Journal of Psychology*, 60, 1–29.
15. For example, D. McClelland, J. Atkinson, R. Clark and E. Lowell, *The Achievement Motive*, New York, Appleton/ Century/Crofts, 1953.
16. Brickman, P. and Campbell , D.T. (1971) Hedonic Relativism and Planning the Good Society, in M.H. Appley (Ed.), *Adaptation-level Theory: A Symposium*, New York, Academic Press, 207–302.

CHAPTER 4

The Calculus of Desire

Abstract In the first half of the eighteenth century, Daniel Bernoulli introduced a major innovation in the study of decision-making. In many respects, his key ideas anticipated Fechner's Law of sensation in the domain of economic decisions. The problem of measuring sensations is thus entwined with that of measuring motivations for economic choices. Bernoulli's original insights developed into modern theories of judgement and decision-making. Inspired by several features of psychophysical models, Nobel Prize winner Daniel Kahneman developed Prospect Theory, effectively turning Weber's and Fechner's original intuitions into a law of desire.

Keywords Utility • Diminishing marginal utility • Prospect theory • Risk aversion • Loss aversion • Subjective probability • Choice behaviours

The great Argentinian novelist Jorge Luis Borges taught us that successors create their own precursors. In an essay written in 1951, Borges imagined conducting a study on writers who anticipated Franz Kafka's works.[1] He came up with a list of six different authors, none of whom had anything in common, except for the fact that they all somehow evoke the themes of Kafka. Paradoxically, this shows how it was Kafka, the successor, who created his own precursors. Kafka's works changed our way of reading them,

© The Author(s), under exclusive license to Springer Nature Switzerland AG 2024
N. Bruno, *A Conceptual History of Psychophysics*,
https://doi.org/10.1007/978-3-031-66597-4_4

defining a network of relations that would never have existed without him. Borges taught us something fundamental about our relationship with the past, and if he is right, then we should not be surprised if the same principle also applies to Weber's Law.

As already mentioned in the introduction, Weber and Fechner's ideas were anticipated by Swiss mathematician Daniel Bernoulli,[2] the father of the economic concept of "utility", over a century earlier. However, Bernoulli developed his ideas starting from problems that were completely different from the study of sensory systems. In fact, he worked on problems that had brought mathematicians to the gambling tables where eighteenth century gentlemen enjoyed waging on many different things. Nonetheless, his ideas were destined to become the foundation of an actual calculus of desire. They informed a psychological theory that aimed to account for the factors that guide our choices in many spheres of human action.

The First Mouthful of Beer

In the first half of the eighteenth century, Daniel Bernoulli introduced a major innovation into the study of decision-making in conditions of uncertainty,[3] a topic dear to the eighteenth century courts due to its applications to gambling. Let's suppose that, in a game, we have to choose between two wagers: in the first we can win €100, in the second only €50. But the first wager is risky, as it has a 40% probability of winning, while the second is less so: here, the probability of winning is 80%. Prior to Bernoulli, mathematicians thought that this problem had to be tackled according to the rules of the game, without considering the characteristics of the decision-maker.[4] Using this "objective" approach, the two wagers have the same value, as the expectations of winning are identical when we weigh the possible gains against the probability of achieving them (40% of €100 = 80% of €50 = €40 in both cases). For Bernoulli, on the other hand, the decision is ultimately subjective, and for this reason cannot be separated from the characteristics of the person expressing it and the circumstances in which it is expressed. Bernoulli therefore hypothesised that decisions are not taken by comparing the objective expected gain but are rather based on the sensation of satisfaction that such gain would give to the person if they won. This sensation is the subjective value of that expected gain, i.e., its "utility" (Bernoulli didn't use this term but this is what was later adopted by economists).

Supporting the distinction between expected gain and utility, Bernoulli started from common sense. For instance, he wrote that a gift of 10 ducats offered to someone with a wealth of 20 ducats corresponds to a very different utility to that of the same gift offered to someone with a wealth of 1000 ducats. In the first case, 10 ducats are 50% of their wealth, a significant part; in the second, they are only 1%, perhaps not negligible yet certainly not noteworthy. He formalised this idea in three principles: that utility should be distinguished from objective value, that changes in utility are some increasing function of changes in objective value, and that changes in utility are an inverse function of absolute objective value.[5] Based on these principles, Bernoulli proposed a logarithmic function as a model of how utility should vary along with the variation in monetary cost.

Of course, monetary cost is something very different from the intensity of a physical quantity, but Bernoulli's idea and his function of utility are the same as Fechner's. If changes in utility are inversely proportional to monetary value, it is like saying that the greater the initial wealth, the greater the increase in money required to make us note an increase in utility. The utility curve must therefore be negatively accelerated, as in the case of Fechner's Law. It was the first formulation of that which economists would later call the law of *diminishing marginal utility*. Diminishing marginal utility is the reason why, as the philosopher of miniscule pleasures Philippe Delerm taught us, the first mouthful of beer is the only one that matters.[6] The pleasure of the first mouthful is intense, long-lasting, and satisfying in moderate quantities. In the subsequent mouthfuls, however, we drink more and more with increasingly less pleasure. If you don't like beer, the same goes for the first slice of cake, your first kiss, and many other things besides. It is a very general principle, and as traders well know, it is a part of all our economic choices.

Let's consider a hypothetical scenario, we will call scenario A. Mr Smith is about to buy a car that costs €30,100. A friend tells him that another dealer is selling the same car for €30,000, but can't remember which one. To find the dealer, it would take Mr Smith at least an hour. Should he find out, or buy the car from the dealer he knows? Now consider a different scenario, scenario B: Mr Jones is about to buy a mobile phone that costs €250. A friend tells him that the same phone is on sale in another shop for €200, but can't remember which one, and again it would take Mr Jones at least an hour to find out. What do you think, will he look for it or buy the phone in the shop he knows already? If you are like me, and like the vast majority of people asked, in scenario A, you will have answered no, but in scenario B, yes.[7] Considered in terms of expected gain, these answers are unreasonable, because in the first case you could save €100, and in the second only €50. But if we consider them in relation to their subjective utility, the answers are quite comprehensible. Compared to a cost of €30,100, an extra €100 in your pocket is not much, a tiny fraction of a percent. But compared to a cost of €250, €50 is quite a large amount, a 20% gain. And of course, all this is nothing other than Weber's Law, applied to the desirability of an economic choice.

Fechner was well aware of Bernoulli's work, and indeed mentioned him in the first few pages of *Elemente*. But Fechner's approach had an advantage over that of Bernoulli, because Fechner's work was based on an empirical fact, Weber's Law, while the starting point for the mathematisation proposed by Bernoulli was based on assumptions. In addition, Fechner developed empirical methods for measuring thresholds, studying discrimination capacity, and building a psychophysical function. Other researchers went on to develop these methods in different directions, in any case compatible with his pioneering insights. The conceptual innovation introduced by Bernoulli, on the other hand, was underestimated by economists for over a century,[8] at least in part, I presume, precisely due to the problems associated with measuring utility. It was only with the development of psychophysics in the second half of the nineteenth century that economists realised what was implicit in Bernoulli's analysis. That is to say, that utility can be thought of as the intensity of the sensation of satisfaction procured by an object/asset. The conceptual framework of psychophysics, designed to mathematicise sensory responses in perception tasks, could thus be applied to the problem of which of two or more alternatives will appear more desirable in many other walks of life.

A Bird in the Hand Is Worth Two in the Bush

Many popular proverbs warn us against uncertain prospects. Better the devil you know than the devil you don't, that is, a certain outcome is always more desirable than an uncertain alternative, at least according to popular wisdom. But is this really true?

In the modern financial world, this attitude is known as *risk aversion,* and risk aversion is deeply rooted in our psychology. Imagine the following situation: you are looking for a job and are called to an interview by two companies. The first offers a salary of €1000 a month, the second a salary of €2100. The job is the same, and the companies are quite similar.

But there is a problem. You find out that the first company usually hires all the people it interviews, while the second usually hires only around 50%. And to make things even more complicated, the job is in the city where you live, but the interviews are on the same day in two cities that are far apart, making it impossible to go to both.

The dilemma is this: what is more desirable, €1000 a month for sure, or €2100 perhaps, running the significant risk of remaining unemployed for who knows how long? Faced with this kind of alternative, most people prefer not to risk. The decision is irrational, because in the second case, if we weigh the monetary value of the alternative with its probability, the expected gain is 50% of €2100 + 50% of 0 = €1050—which is more than the €1000 offered by the first company. In other words, it would be rational for a decision-maker to run this risk.

What does risk aversion depend on? On many things, of course, and we are all a bit different. But one thing is clear: a key component of risk aversion is the shape of the subjective value curve. If the curve is concave (negatively accelerated, like Fechner's function and as proposed by Bernoulli), there must be risk aversion. Figure 4.1 shows the curve that describes how the subjective value changes (in the same way as sensation in Fechner's function) as the monetary value of the salary changes. To find the value of the salary offered by the first company, €1000, move upwards from that point on the *x*-axis to meet the curve, and then move sideways to the corresponding value on the *y*-axis. The same goes for the value of the salary offered by the second company, €2100, which obviously has a higher subjective value as the curve grows continuously. But in this case the salary of the second company is uncertain, as we also have to consider the other possibility, that we may not be hired after the interview.

The subjective value of the risky choice is therefore the sum of the subjective values associated with the alternatives (€2100 and €0) multiplied by their probability (50%). In the figure, this is half-way on the *y*-axis between zero and the subjective value of €2100, which is below the subjective value associated with €1000. Therefore, a person whose value curve resembles that shown in Fig. 4.1 has to be averse to risk.

If you think about it, this kind of person should refuse a risky choice even if this had exactly the same value as the safe choice. Which of these two alternatives seems most desirable: receiving €10, or tossing a coin: heads, you win €20, tails, you get nothing. Assuming the coin isn't rigged (probability of heads = 50%), the expected gain of the wager is the same as the value of the certain offer. If you repeat the wager many times, in the

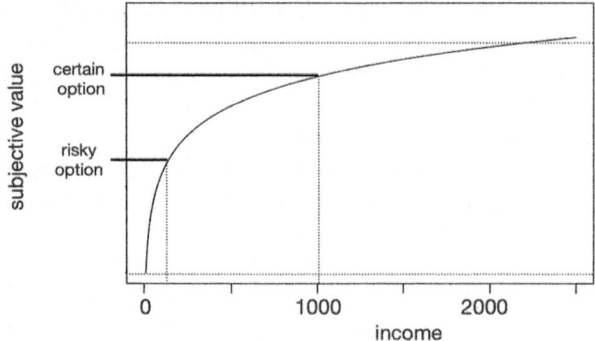

Fig. 4.1 The phenomenon of risk aversion is explained by the concave shape (similar to that of Fechner's function) of the curve. You can see that the subjective value of the risky choice corresponds to the sum of the subjective values of the two options (2100 Euros or nothing, dotted horizontal lines) multiplied by their probability (50%). Note that this value lies exactly half-way between the subjective value of a €2100 salary and a €0 salary, if these were certain. For this reason, the subjective value of the risky choice, for a person whose curve has this shape, becomes much less than that of the safe choice

end you win €20 for half the tosses, and so win an average of €10 for each toss. But given that the value curve is concave, also in this case the sum of the subjective values associated with the two alternatives (€20 and €0) multiplied by their probability (50%) is less than the subjective value of €10. The risky alternative appears less desirable.

This goes for most people, but not all. In fact, people have different attitudes to risk: some of us are more or less inclined to risk, others have a more neutral attitude. What is interesting, however, is that at this point we have a mathematical instrument for describing the difference between such individuals.

For those averse to risk, the curve must be concave, like the one in Fig. 4.1. For those inclined to risk, on the other hand, it must be convex. Finally, for those with a neutral attitude, the "curve" must lie half way, i.e., it must be a straight line. In this case, the subjective value will be equal to the monetary value. Figure 4.2 represents these three types of attitude to risk. At least in qualitative terms, this three-part classification recalls the three types of psychophysical curve described by Stevens (Fig. 2.3). The fundamental distinction between the desirability of safety, at the price of a

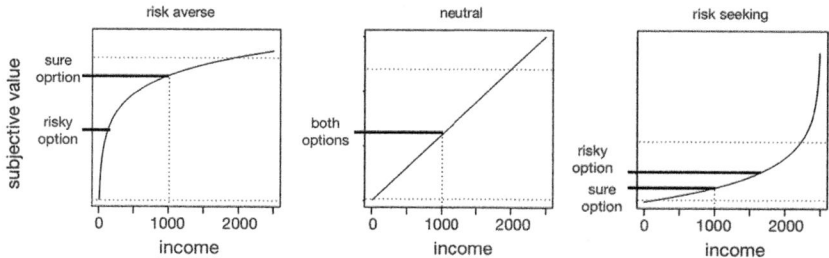

Fig. 4.2 Three types of attitude to risk shown by three types of subjective value curve. Suppose you have to choose between two alternatives with the same expected salary: a sure salary of €1000 and a salary of €2000 with a probability of 50%. With a concave curve, the subjective value of the risky option lies below that of the safe option. A person with this attitude will be averse to risk. With a straight line, the subjective value of the risky option is equal to the monetary value. This person is indifferent to the two options. With a convex curve, the subjective value of the risky option lies above that of the safe option. This person is inclined to risk

mediocre payoff, and that of a greater payoff running the risk of a negative event, can be conceptually described in a similar way to the distinction between different types of sensory systems.

The Dark Side of Desire

In 2011, videomaker Derek Muller set up a highly successful YouTube channel, *Veritasium*.[9] In my opinion, *Veritasium* is one of the best examples of the use of new media for scientific popularisation. In one of the episodes, Muller interviews random individuals on the street, offering them the chance to take part in a very simple game. Toss a coin, heads I give you 10 dollars, tails you give me 10 dollars. As shown in the video, no one is willing to take part, giving various excuses: I don't like gambling, I don't want to give you 10 dollars, and so on. This is surprising, as the game (in contrast to the typical gambling games you find in a casino) is, in all simplicity, completely honest. The two participants have the same probability of winning or losing each time the coin is tossed, and in the long run nobody wins or loses (i.e., the expected gain for both players is zero). Muller then raises the stakes: heads I give you 12, 15, or 20 dollars, tails you still give me 10. But nothing changes: nobody wants to play. Raising the stakes even higher, somebody starts to show some interest, although one woman says that she wouldn't play even if she were offered 100 dollars. And this is even more bizarre, because all these new versions of the game are to the interviewees' advantage, in some cases considerably so.

The video demonstrates the existence of a phenomenon called *loss aversion*. If we compare two alternatives, one of which is a gain (I win 10 dollars) and the other a loss (I lose 10 dollars), the psychological effect of the potential loss is far stronger than that of the gain. The monetary value is always the same, the only difference being that in one case we take away and in the other we add. However, the possibility of losing is very aversive. For some of us, even doubling the amount of the gain is not enough to compensate how much we *do not want* to lose. All in all, the dark side of desire is far more powerful than its light side.

Loss aversion was discovered by two Israeli psychologists (who both taught in the USA), Amos Tversky and Daniel Kahneman. Tversky and Kahneman used this discovery to develop a theory of decision-making in conditions of uncertainty known as *Prospect Theory*. This theory is considered one of the most important scientific contributions to both decision psychology and behavioural economics and finance. And, as I mentioned in the first chapter, in 2012, Kahneman received the Nobel Prize for Economics. As we will see below, prospect theory explains loss aversion by exploiting ideas inspired by the psychophysics of Weber, Fechner, and Helson.

As Kahneman wrote in a successful essay,[10] the first seeds of the theory began to germinate around 50 years ago, in the first half of the 1960s. At that time, Tversky and Kahneman had begun investigating the psychology of decision-making, particularly focusing on decisions made in conditions of uncertainty. In theoretical terms, a natural starting point was risk aversion in the context of the subjective value model proposed by Bernoulli. As explained in the previous paragraph, risk aversion is explained convincingly by the fact that the subjective value curve is concave. But there's another problem. In Bernoulli's model, the subjective value is an absolute measurement calculated in relation to a starting point with zero value (and here note the analogy with the earlier discussion of absolute thresholds). In other words, the subjective value of an object can simply be found starting from the corresponding monetary value, if we know the shape of the curve.

Tversky and Kahneman, however, realised that things didn't work in this way. For instance, let's suppose that both Jack and Jill now have a wealth of €5 million. In Bernoulli's model, the subjective value of their assets is exactly the same. But if I tell you that last week Jack had €9 million, and Jill just €1 million? Is it plausible that the subjective value of €5 million is the same for both? Of course not. Jack will be unhappy about a drastic reduction, while Jill will be very pleased with a significant increase. Working with examples like this, Tversky and Kahneman realised that the subjective value of a sum of money cannot be calculated in absolute terms, as it depends on how this has changed compared to initial wealth. The analogy with the concept of adaptation level in psychophysics is clear. In the same way that, in the psychophysics of sensory systems, the effect of a stimulus has to be assessed in relation to the adaptation level, the effect of a monetary value must be assessed in relation to initial wealth.

The two researchers realised that these observations could be used to predict differences in risk aversion, depending on the reference point characterising a decision. They therefore started to work on situations like the following. Let's suppose that Jack and Jill are facing the same dilemma. What is more desirable, a safe investment, which after a year gives them both a wealth of €2 million (safe option), or investing in a portfolio of shares which, according to current estimates, after one year could give them a return of between €1 and €4 million (risky option)? If the estimates are correct, without additional information it is probable that the investment in shares will give them assets worth €2.5 million, the average value of the estimates, but we can never be sure of this. Global markets could do badly, and then both will find themselves with only €1 million, or markets could do well and their return could even reach €4 million.

There is no way of knowing, and this is precisely the essence of decision-making in conditions of uncertainty. The situation is similar to that shown in Fig. 4.1. It is as if Jack and Jill both had to choose between a sure return of €2 million, on one hand, and €1 or €4 million with a 50% probability. If Jack and Jill are similarly risk-averse, Bernoulli's theory expects both of them to choose the sure option, even if this will lead to a much lower gain than what they might earn with the risky option. As the curve is concave, the sum of the subjective values of these last two sums, weighed with their probability, will be less than the subjective value of the sure amount.

But now imagine that Jack's current wealth is €1 million. Compared to this point of reference, Jack's dilemma is: is it better to double his wealth for sure, or to try to quadruple it, running the significant risk of not earning even a Euro? It's not hard to imagine that Jack might be risk-averse. And on the other hand, imagine that Jill's wealth is €4 million. She is facing a very different dilemma: is it better to lose half her wealth for sure, or run the risk of losing three quarters of her wealth, but with a very strong possibility of not losing anything? In these conditions, it would not be surprising if Jill preferred to risk.

And this is where Bernoulli's theory is lacking. If subjective value is calculated in relation to current assets, in psychological terms all the variations are coloured by emotions. For Jack, it is a matter of choosing between two prospective gains, and this makes him averse to risk. For Jill, on the other hand, it is a matter of choosing between two prospective losses, and this changes everything. It is highly plausible that Jill will be inclined to risk. This is exactly the new element characterising prospect theory, compared to the previous attempts to forecast choice behaviours.

In prospect theory, risk aversion occurs when the decision takes place in a context of gains. In a context of losses, the opposite occurs: people become inclined to risk. Tversky and Kahneman show how their theory works with a graph (Fig. 4.3) which, not by chance, is similar to the graphs illustrating psychophysical functions in Chap. 2. Just like Bernoulli's curve, the graph shows the change in subjective value according to the change in monetary value. Yet, there are three major differences.

Firstly, the change in subjective value is calculated in relation to a reference value, i.e., an adaptation level, which depends on the context and many other things, and which changes over time. The monetary value must therefore always be a decrease or increase in relation to this reference, defining a loss-gain axis according to which the subjective value decreases or increases, defining a disappointment-satisfaction axis. This means that the function is defined in two of the four possible quadrants, those in which the portions of the axes are both positive or both negative.

Secondly, both curves are shaped consistently with those of Fechner and Bernoulli. In the gains quadrant, subjective value grows as a function of monetary gains as a negatively accelerated curve. The same is true, in general terms, in the losses quadrant, except that now the value is reduced, in relation to the reference, as losses increase. The result is an S-shaped curve (not to be confused with the curve that describes thresholds). If you look closely, however, you will see that the sigmoid is not symmetrical: if we rotated one of the two around the x-axis, they would not overlap perfectly. The subjective value increases in the positive quadrant more slowly than it decreases in the negative quadrant.

The shape of the curve in the gains quadrant explains the reason why, if we consider two job offers, the one that offers us an increase from €1000

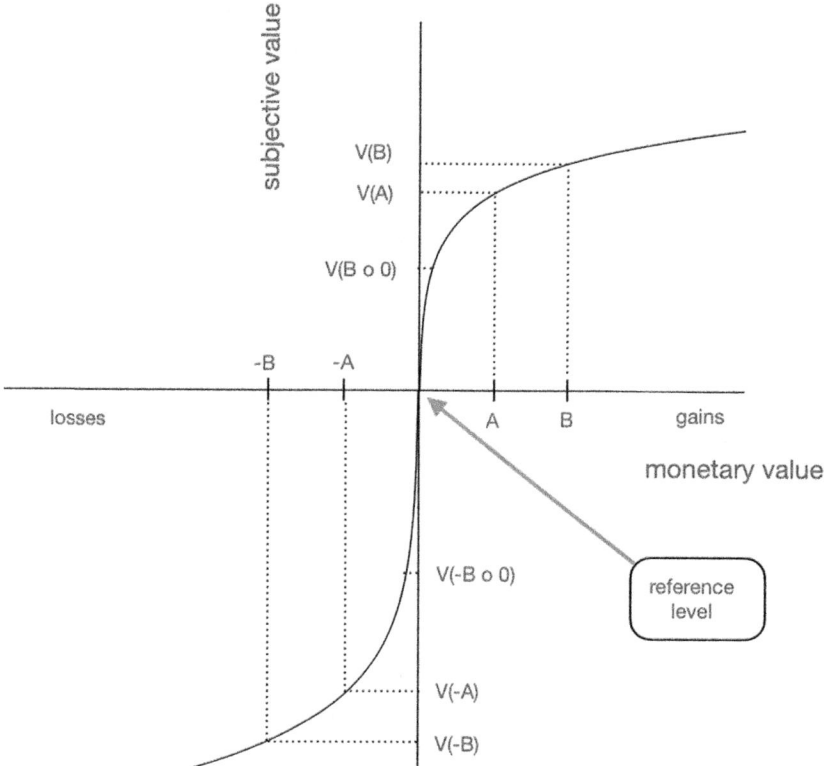

Fig. 4.3 Prospect theory. Subjective value is a sigmoid function of monetary value, but disappointment grows faster in the negative quadrant of the plot than satisfaction increases in the positive quadrant. Note that (1) the satisfaction associated with an increase from the reference level to B is only slightly higher than the increase from the reference to A (Weber's Law); (2) the disappointment associated with losing −A is higher, as an absolute value, than the satisfaction associated with gaining A (loss aversion); (3) a certain disadvantageous outcome V(A) has higher subjective value than a risky alternative V(B or 0) in which one may gain B or nothing (risk aversion in a gain context); (4) the subjective disappointment associated to a risky alternative V(−B or 0) is less than that of a certain outcome V(−A) (risk propensity in a loss context)

to €2000 seems almost the same as the one that offers an increase from €1000 to €2100 (a significant 5% in monetary terms, but a minimum increase in terms of subjective value). This is none other than Weber's Law, the major difference being that the curve would begin at €1000 rather than at zero.

Moreover, again in the gains quadrant, the shape of the curve explains why we prefer a disadvantageous sure option to a potentially more advantageous but uncertain one. This is risk aversion. As we saw in the previous paragraph, this phenomenon depends on the concave shape of the subjective value curve. But this alone is not enough. Comparing gains and losses, we realise that in a loss context, risk aversion may turn into risk propensity: if I have two uncertain losses, once their probabilities are taken into account the subjective pain is less than that associated with a sure loss.

Finally, the shape of the curve explains why, in the game Derek Muller proposed in *Veritasium*, people refuse a wager in which, if it's heads, they win €10 and if it's tails they lose €10. This is loss aversion. Due to the asymmetrical shape of the *S*, the disappointment of paying €10 is far more intense than the pleasure or receiving €10. A much higher gain would be needed to compensate for the asymmetry.

Lady Luck in the Mind

In the situations described above, we considered how a person might decide which of two future alternatives is the more desirable. We also saw how, in prospect theory, these decisions depend on the psychological impact of a change in relation to a benchmark level. In classic subjective value theory, from Bernoulli onwards, psychological impact is estimated by weighing the possible alternatives with their probability, as we did with the previous examples. In investigating this aspect of the theory, Tversky and Kahneman realised that here too lies a problem.

Let's look at one example Kahneman often used. Suppose you have the chance to win €1 million, and that you are in a situation where you can increase the probability of this win by 5%. Now compare three versions of this hypothetical situation: (a) the probability increases from 0 to 5%; (b) the probability increases from 60 to 65%; (c) the probability increases from 95 to 100%. According to the classic theory, in all three cases, the psychological impact is given by the subjective value of €1 million, multiplied by the probability of 5%. Do you think it is plausible that a person would treat the three alternatives in the same way? Clearly, increases from

0 to 5% and from 95 to 100% affect us differently from the intermediate increase of 60 to 65%. The first and last are qualitative changes: in the first case, from the impossibility to the possibility of an event occurring; in the last, from possibility to certainty. Psychologically speaking, the first and last are situations whereby a 5% increase introduces certainty into a previously uncertain context. The second case is a mere quantitative reduction of uncertainty. The observation was interesting, and the two researchers realised that it suggested a way of solving some difficulties in their theory.

One of the most important innovations of prospect theory, also in practical terms, is the asymmetry of the sigmoid curve and its implications for loss aversion. Due to the different shape of the two halves of the sigmoid curve, people tend to overestimate the disappointment of a loss compared to the pleasure of a gain. They tend to, but with some major exceptions. Consider, for instance, when people decide to play the lottery. Suppose a lottery ticket costs €10 and the prize is €1 million. Here, the player's dilemma is to spend €10 and have practically zero possibility of €1 million, or €0 with a probability that touches certainty. The prospect of losing €10 should be aversive. And, on the other hand, the probability of winning €1 million is so small that it makes the subjective value of this risky gain almost zero. Thus, one would predict that people keep their €10, but nonetheless many people buy lottery tickets.

To solve this problem, prospect theory proposes that when making decisions, the subjective value takes into account not the mathematical probability but rather subjective estimates of probability, which Tversky and Kahneman called "decision weights". In some cases, these subjective estimates are quite similar to mathematical probability, but in others they are far different. Very small probabilities particularly tend to be overestimated, because their psychological impact is influenced by a qualitative change. As is the case of an increase from 0 to 5% probability, a desirable event changes from impossible to possible, even if improbable. Tversky and Kahneman called this systematic error in the subjective estimation of a probability the "possibility effect", which explains why people lose money playing the lottery. The subjective value of the win, weighed with a highly overestimated subjective probability, becomes greater than the subjective negative value of the cost of the lottery ticket.

It does however explain many other behaviours, at least in part. Think, for example, of Professor Unrat, the lead character in Heinrich Mann's[11] novel and in the film that made Marlene Dietrich famous, *Die Blaue Engel* ("The Blue Angel"). Or think of Humbert-Humbert, the protagonist of the extraordinary novel by Vladimir Nabokov, *Lolita*.[12] Both are mature men who fall in love with a much younger woman, and revolutionise their lives in the unrealistic expectation of being able to keep her for themselves. We could say that they both buy an expensive lottery ticket, having for a series of reasons overestimated the probability of winning, and with tragic outcomes.

Another major difference between decision weights and mathematical probability is the underestimation of very high probabilities. In this case, the qualitative change corresponds to the passage from uncertainty to certainty, as in the increase from 95 to 100%. This is a *certainty effect*, which explains why, in a gain context, people become even more averse to risk if the probability of a positive outcome is very high. Think about this situation: you have taken legal action to recover a debt of €10,000, and the lawyer estimates that there is a 95% probability that the judge will order the debtor to pay. However, the legal system is unpredictable, and there is always a chance that you will not win the case. The debtor offers a transaction: he is willing to pay you €8500 to settle the matter out of court. In this situation, many people would accept the settlement, even though the expected gain of the risky option is €9500, much higher than the amount offered for the settlement. Risk aversion is always part of a gain context due to the concave shape of the curve. But in this case, it is amplified by the underestimation of the probability of winning the case, making the subjective value of the uncertain event less than the objectively unfavourable certain event.

The certainty effect also explains why, in a loss context, people become more inclined to risk if the probability of a disastrous outcome is very high. These are situations in which a failure that could have been managed turns into a catastrophe. For instance, think of a compulsive gambler who, having already lost a considerable amount, rather than cutting his losses and leaving, continues to gamble until he has lost everything he owns, in the unrealistic hope of winning it all back again. Or, again, think of a company with severe losses that is by now practically out of business, but continues to spend the little resources it still has in the futile attempt to get back on its feet. In these cases, the context is that of losses, and the probability of an even greater loss is very high. Accepting the situation would seem to be the only rational thing to do. But as very high probabilities are underestimated, the hope of a stroke of luck in order to recover prevails, in addition to the risk propensity implicit in a loss context.

SHOULD I STAY, OR SHOULD I GO?

The force of desire guides our economic decisions. Often, however, the decisions that count most in our lives are not economic. In a past academic year, I asked a group of students attending a series of lectures on the psychology of reasoning to anonymously indicate the three most important decisions they had had to take in their lives. I was struck by the results. Almost all the answers concerned dilemmas such as: continuing to live with their parents or begin a life on their own; going to university in their home town or in a different city; continuing their relationship with their partner or ending it.

What I found interesting was not so much the type of decisions in the list, which presumably reflected the age of the interviewees, but rather the type of juxtaposition they suggested. If I had repeated the same operation with a group of 40-somethings I am sure that the dilemmas would have been different: having a child or forgoing parenthood; getting married or staying single; living in a rented property or buying a house; staying with their current employer or changing job. Important decisions in our lives often have this "should I stay or should I go" structure. There are lots of factors that make a change more desirable, and of course these depend on our individual stories, goals, or the opportunities we are offered. However, prospect theory can help us to understand the role of fundamental psychological mechanisms[13] that affect all of us to some extent and provide us with the tools to measure the intensity of this influence.

The decision to stay is one in favour of the *status quo*, the situation we are currently in and which we are somehow familiar with. The decision to go is one that moves in an uncertain direction, which may have positive outcomes, but there is also a risk that the outcomes might turn out negative. In many of these cases, risk aversion can play a key role. Furthermore, depending on the context, the alternatives can appear to us as losses or gains. The theory states that the potential pain of loss should prevail over the potential pleasure of an equivalent gain, thus leading us towards a conservative choice. This is loss aversion, which depends on the shape of the S curve of subjective value.

Loss aversion is one of the reasons why some of us remain stuck in a "toxic" relationship with an unsuited or depreciating partner, without being able to find the strength to end it. The prospect of losing what we have—economic security, social status, a home—is more aversive than the prospect of gaining in tranquillity and new opportunities. In extreme cases, when a male partner is also violent, this can have tragic consequences. If a man is responsible for repeated episodes of violence, it is probable that he will continue to be so, even though these men often swear that they will never do it again. But the tendency to underestimate very high probabilities makes the prospect of more violent episodes relatively less important, and the loss aversion continues to prevail, often leading the victim to justify their partner's actions and overestimate their presumed positive qualities.

The result threatens not only the victim's physical integrity but also their mental health. A recent study by a mixed group of Korean and US researchers[14] observed higher levels of risk aversion and loss aversion in a group of patients suffering from severe depression and a history of attempted suicide, compared to a control group without symptoms of depression. Using functional magnetic resonance, the same study also observed anomalies in the neural responses to loss or gain prospects in the cingulate cortex, the insula, and the amygdala, regions of the brain that are involved in the assessment and regulation of emotions. In this way, the calculus of desire carried out using tools deriving from psychophysics is confirmed by the data collected using cognitive neuroscience techniques.

What is perhaps even more interesting, however, are studies investigating the starting point of a relationship rather than its end. What makes a person desirable as a potential romantic partner and, perhaps even more important, what makes him or her undesirable? In a series of elegant studies,[15] the US researcher Peter Jonason, currently teaching at the University of Padua, examined in detail which characteristics and personality traits lead people to choose not to start a relationship after a first date, or to change an initially positive impression into a negative one after the initial courting stages. The results highlight not only obvious individual differences but also differences according to the time perspective: in short-term relationships, physical aspects prevail, along with the state of health and personal care. In long-term relationships, on the other hand, personality traits and lifestyle take centre stage.

These differences can be interpreted in terms of evolutionary biology. The aim of short-term relationships is often to satisfy a more hedonic desire, also in intimate terms. With long-term relationships, desire shifts more towards a life project and building a family. However, in relation to the subject of this book, the interesting thing here is the effect of "push" factors in comparison with the corresponding effect of "pull" factors. The former negatively affect decision-making far more than the latter push us in the direction of a positive decision. This result is consistent with prospect theory. The prospect of a future failure of the relationship becomes a loss contest, such that the subjective negative value of this prospect is more averse than the subjective value associated with a potential success.

Notes

1. J.L. Borges, *Kafka y sus precursores*, in *Otras inquisiciones*, Buenos Aires, Sur, 1952; English translation, *Kafka and His Precursors*, in *Other Inquisitions*, University of Texas Press, 1964.
2. Daniel Bernoulli (1700–1782) is considered one of the most brilliant mathematicians and physicists of modern times. He made fundamental scientific contributions to the field of fluid dynamics, the theory of probability and statistics. My claim that Bernoulli anticipated Weber and Fechner is bound to be controversial. Experts in sensory psychophysics will likely raise two objections. First, Bernoulli did not start from Weber's Law in his mathematical derivation. Second, utility and sensation are different things. In my opinion, however, the conceptual connection between Bernoulli, Weber, and Fechner is apparent. Concerning the first objection, I note that the general principles upon which Bernoulli derived his theory essentially boil down to the idea that the psychological effect of increases in objective value is inversely proportional to the corresponding starting value—which is essentially Weber's Law applied to economics. Concerning the second objection, I note that one of Bernoulli's most important innovations was the distinction between objective value, the price of goods, and utility or subjective value, the psychological satisfaction provided by goods. Utility is thus a mental content, just like sensation is. Bernulli's model may be regarded as psychophysics applied to the social rather than the physical environment.
3. The essay entitles *Specimen Theoriae Novae de Mensura Sortis* ("Exposition of a New Theory on the Measurement of Risk"), published by Bernoulli in 1738 at the St. Petersburg Academy of Sciences is today considered one of the fundamental texts on the theory of utility in economics.
4. In particular, between the late seventeenth and early eighteenth centuries, Christiaan Huygens, Pierre Rèmond de Montmort and Abraham de Moivre introduced concepts like "expected value" to the study of the outcome of a gambling game. Their works contributed significantly to the development of the modern theory of probability.
5. Masin, S.C., Zudini, V. and Antonelli, M. (2009) Early alternative derivations of Fechner's Law. *Journal of the history of the behavioral sciences*, 45, 56–65.
6. P. Delerm, *Le première gorgée de bière – et autres plaisirs minuscules*, Paris, Éditions Gallimard, 2012; English translation: *The Small Pleasures of Life*, London, W&N, 2018.

7. Don't worry if you gave a different answer. Choices like these depend on many factors, including the familiarity with the situations described in the scenarios, your income, the fact that you are reading this book, the value you give to time, and, most importantly, the fact that the two scenarios should be presented to separate groups of participants to check for order effects that may influence the answers.
8. On the reception of Bernoulli's essay among nineteenth-century economists, see Giocoli, N. (1998). The "True" Hypothesis of Daniel Bernoulli: What Did the Marginalists Really Know? *History of Economic Ideas*, 6, pp. 7–43.
9. Born in Australia, Muller grew up in Canada and currently works in the United States. After graduating in Engineering, Muller obtained a PhD in Pedagogy of Physics and worked in both cinema and television. *Veritasium* is a neologism combining the Latin word *veritas* with the suffix used in English for many chemical elements (e.g., *gallium*). It therefore means "an element of truth". The channel presents short videos on fundamental scientific concepts, with very interesting and entertaining demonstrations and exceptionally clear explanations. The channel became a huge critical success and is especially appreciated by the public. At the time of writing, the video described in the text has been viewed by over 7 million visitors.
10. Kahneman, D. (2012). *Thinking, Fast and Slow*, London, Penguin Random House. For the same reasons as Bernoulli's, my attempt to connect Kahneman's prospect theory to psychophysics is bound to be controversial. I note, however, that Kahneman himself worked in psychophysics at the beginning of his career. See for instance Kahneman D, Norman J, Kubovy M. (1967) Critical duration for the resolution of form: centrally or peripherally determined? *Journal of Experimental Psychology*, 73, 323–7.
11. Mann, H. (1979). *The Blue Angel*, New York: F. Ungar. Heinrich was the elder brother of the even more famous Thomas Mann, who won the Nobel Prize for Literature in 1929.
12. Nabokov, V.V. (2000). *Lolita*, Penguin Classics.
13. See for instance Gilovich, T. (1991) *How we know what isn't so: The fallibility of human reason in everyday life*. New York: The free press.
14. Baek, K. , Kown, J., Chae, J. et al. (2017). Heightened Aversion to Risk and Loss in Depressed Patients with a Suicide Attempt History, *Scientific Reports*, 7, 11228, https://doi.org/10.1038/s41598-017-10541-5.
15. See Jonason, P.K., Garcia, J. , Webster, G. et al. (2015) Relationship Dealbreakers: Traits People Avoid in Potential Mates. *Personality and Social Psychology Bulletin*, 4, 1697–1711; Jonason, P.K., White, K.P. and Al-Shawaf, L. (2020) Should I Stay or Should I Go: Individual Differences in Response to Romantic Dealmakers and Dealbreakers, *Personality and Individual Differences*, 164, 110120.

CHAPTER 5

Epilogue

Abstract In conclusion, some reflections on the challenges and decisions involved in writing this book. I underscore the significance of psychophysics in psychological, neuroscientific, and economic theories, highlighting the pervasive influence of Weber's Law in contemporary contexts such as marketing, product design, and behavioural economics.

Keywords Naturalization of mind • Mental "organs"

And so we have reached the end. One of the hardest things for anyone writing a book like this is deciding which topics to include and which to leave aside. I found myself facing this problem both in the description of the mathematical models marking the evolution of Weber's ideas from the nineteenth century to modern times and in the choice of which practical examples to include.

As concerns the first aspect, I tried to focus on the concepts that were indispensable for understanding the history of this evolution, both with reference to the role of psychophysics in psychology and neurosciences and to its role in economic theories. For the latter, I must admit that there would be many more interesting things to say. For instance, the role of Weber's Law in marketing is well-established since at least 50 years.[1] Fechnerian psychophysics is used in product design[2] and in assessing behavioural deficits in neurological patients.[3] Prospect theory has been used to study the choices made by overweight people having to follow a diet,[4] the behaviour of adolescents in relation to the prevention of sexually transmitted diseases,[5] and as a starting point for the selection of a portfolio of financial investments.[6] In our contemporary world, psychophysics is everywhere, and for this Weber's Law has every right to be considered a key formula for reading the world.

It may seem strange that an idea, and a mathematical model, born in the nineteenth century to study the physiology and psychology of sensory organs have become a model of desire in economics and in the psychology of contemporary decision-making. For some, perhaps, this is also unsatisfactory. When we think of our sensations, and in particular of the desire we feel towards certain things or certain life prospects, it is only natural to want to know more about the nature of these contents of our mental life.

But remember what we said at the start of the book. The purpose of these models is not to reveal the essence of desire, but rather to identify the functional relations between changes in these experiences and changes in external and internal stimuli that are processed mentally to become conscious experiences. To be honest, for many scientists desire is in fact none other than that complex network of relations, and there is nothing identifiable in our brains that we could label as "desire". There is instead a complex network of mostly unconscious mental mechanisms that ultimately account for our experience. This is perhaps the real dark side of desire, a side we can understand only indirectly, using the methods put at our disposal today by psychology and cognitive neuroscience. Here, however, the discourse would spill over into intricate problems in the philosophy of mind. What really counts is that these models allow us to forecast how people will respond to a set of stimuli, and to measure their responses.

For others, a reason for dissatisfaction could derive from what we might describe as insufficient attention to our individuality. We think of desire as something idiosyncratic, built according to our personality and our life story, and it would be unrealistic to deny that, in fact, that's the way things are. Desire is always also modulated by our individual characteristics. But for scientific psychology and the cognitive neurosciences, the object of interest is not what stands us apart from our conspecifics, but rather what we all have in common in how our minds work.

This is basically the point. As with a cardiologist who, to understand the origins of a disease, must firstly consider the general principles governing the functioning of a typical heart, those who study mental function are first and foremost interested in understanding how mental faculties like perception, memory, attention, and so on actually work, in all of us, whatever our individual differences. These differences then become important for understanding why dysfunctions in these faculties occur, and for finding effective treatments, but these are the domains of clinical psychology, neurology, and psychiatry. For those studying basic science, the aim is to know, not to apply knowledge. According to this aim, cognitive functions are studied as mental "organs", defined by biology and the evolutionary history of our species.

This kind of naturalisation of the mind has proved incredibly useful in advancing knowledge. It can be applied to a huge variety of behaviours, from the impact on us of sensory stimuli to the factors that guide our big or everyday decisions and being aware of all this can help us to act more wisely in many situations. For instance, controlling the volume of the music we listen to in our headphones, deciding how to invest our savings, managing our relationship with food, and even, as I have sought to demonstrate, in our sentimental lives. If after having read this book, the way in which you taste the first mouthful of beer will be different to before you read it, I believe that at least in part I will have achieved my goal.

NOTES

1. Britt, S.H. (1975). How Weber's Law Can Be Applied to Marketing, *Business Horizons*, 18, 21–29.
2. Hazfeld, C., Kühner, M., Söllner, S. *et al.*, (2017). Human Perception Measures for Product Design and Development: A Tutorial to Measurement Methods and Analysis, *Multimodal Technologies and Interaction*, 1, 28, https://doi.org/10.3390/mti1040028.
3. Koyama, S. (2008). *Applications of Psychophysics to Neurology*, Brain Nerve, 60, 2008, pp. 463–469.
4. S. Lim, S. and Bruce, A.S. (2015) Prospect Theory and Body Mass: Characterizing Psychological Parameters for Weight-related Risk Attitudes and Weight-gain Aversion, *Frontiers in Psychology*, 6, 330, https://doi.org/10.3389/fpsyg.2015.00330.
5. McDermott, R. (1998) Adolescent HIV Prevention and Intervention: A Prospect Theory Analysis, *Psychology, Health & Medicine*, 3, 371–385.
6. de Giorgi, E. and Hens, T. (2006) Making Prospect Theory Fit for Finance. *Financial Markets and Portfolio Management*, 20, https://doi.org/10.1007/s11408-006-0019-1.

Index[1]

A
Adaptation, 33, 34, 46
Adaptation level, 46, 47, 59, 60

B
Bekesy von, G., 35, 36, 48n7
Bernoulli, D., 3, 52–55, 58–60, 62, 67n2, 67n3, 68n8, 68n10
Blake, W., 8, 32, 36
Borges, J. L., 51, 52, 67n1

C
Certainty effect, 64
Cones, 33, 34
Consciousness, 10, 32, 38, 49n12
Constant stimuli (method), 34

D
Decibel, 16, 17, 26, 29n9
Decision, 2, 3, 47, 49n13, 52, 55, 58–60, 62–65, 67, 71
Decision-making, 3, 5n6, 52, 58, 59, 66, 70
Delerm, P., 53
Desire, 1–3, 4n2, 10, 15, 27, 39, 41, 47, 51–67, 70
Detection, 28n5
Diminishing marginal utility, 53
Discrimination, 10, 11, 14, 27, 28n5, 46, 54

E
External psychophysics, 45

[1] Note: Page numbers followed by 'n' refer to notes.

F

Fechner, G. T., 2, 3, 5n3, 5n5, 9, 12, 13, 15, 20–22, 24–26, 28n5, 28n6, 28–29n8, 33, 34, 36, 40–46, 48n10, 52–56, 58, 60, 67n2

Fechner's Law, 5n5, 13–16, 18–20, 22, 24, 26, 27, 28n6, 28n7, 32, 45, 53

G

Galilei, G., 3, 5n4
Gateless gate, 45–47, 49n12
Gaussian curve, 41, 42, 44

H

Hartline, H. K., 20, 21
Hecht, S., 21, 29n13, 48n8
Hedonic relativism, 47
Helson, H., 46, 47, 58
Hipparchus, 18, 19
Huxley, A., 31, 32, 48n2

I

Intensity, 2, 9, 10, 13, 14, 16–27, 28n5, 28n8, 29n9, 29n13, 32–34, 36–40, 43–46, 53, 54, 65
Internal psychophysics, 45

J

Jnd, just-noticeable difference, 20, 29n11, 36
Jonason, P., 66

K

Kafka, F., 51
Kahneman, D., 3, 5n6, 58–60, 62, 63, 68n10

L

Logarithm, 13, 20
Loss aversion, 58, 61–63, 65, 66

M

MacKay, D., 26, 27
Magnitude estimation (method), 21, 24–26
Magnitude, stars, 18, 19, 29n10
Mann, H., 63, 68n11
Muller, D., 57, 62, 68n9

N

Nabokov, V., 64
Naturalisation of mind, 71

P

Pain scales, 25
Perception, 8, 10, 21, 28n4, 28n7, 54, 71
Phantom vibration, 39, 40, 43, 44
Pirenne, M. H., 32–38, 48n8
Pogson, R., 18, 19
Possibility effect, 63
Probability, 33–35, 38, 40, 41, 43, 44, 49n11, 52, 55–57, 59, 62–64, 66, 67n2, 67n4
Prospect theory, 58, 60–63, 65, 67, 68n10, 70
Psychoanalysis, 2
Psychology, experimental, 2
Psychometric function, 37
Psychophysical function, 22, 23, 28n6, 40, 54, 60
Psychophysics, 2–4, 12, 15, 20, 25–27, 28n5, 29n14, 32, 36–40, 43–47, 48n10, 54, 58, 59, 66, 67n2, 68n10, 69, 70

R

Random error, 38, 39, 41
Relationships, 4n2, 5n3, 10–12, 16, 21, 22, 26, 27, 36, 38, 40, 46, 52, 65–67, 71
Retina, 33–35, 48n6
Risk aversion, 54–56, 58–62, 64–66
Rods, 33–35

S

Sensation, 2, 3, 9, 12–27, 27n3, 28n5, 28n8, 29n11, 32, 36, 39, 40, 42–46, 52, 54, 55, 67n2, 70
Sigmoid, 36, 39, 60, 61, 63
Signal detection theory, 49n13
Sound of silence, 39–45
Standard deviation, 42, 49n11
Stevens' law, 23, 24, 26, 27
Stevens, S. S., 21–27, 29n14, 56

T

Threshold
 absolute, 14, 15, 20, 28n5, 28n7, 32, 34–36, 38, 39, 45, 58
 differential, 28n5, 28n8, 32
Tversky, Amos, 5n6, 58–60, 62, 63

U

Utility, 3, 52–54, 67n2, 67n3

W

Weber, E. H., 2, 3, 5n5, 8, 9, 12, 14, 21, 27n2, 27n3, 28n6, 28–29n8, 46, 48n10, 52, 58, 67n2, 69
Weber's law, 4, 9–15, 20, 21, 28n6, 28–29n8, 52, 54, 61, 62, 67n2, 69, 70
Wixted, J., 32
Wundt, W., 7

Printed by Printforce, the Netherlands